Great Prosecutions

CRIME, JUSTICE, AND PUNISHMENT

Great Prosecutions

Nancy Peacock

Austin Sarat, GENERAL EDITOR

CHELSEA HOUSE PUBLISHERS
Philadelphia

Frontispiece: *The Nuremberg war crimes trials in session, 1946.*

Chelsea House Publishers

Editor in Chief Sally Cheney
Associate Editor in Chief Kim Shinners
Production Manager Pamela Loos
Art Director Sara Davis
Director of Photography Judy L. Hasday

Staff for GREAT PROSECUTIONS

Senior Editor John Ziff
Associate Art Director Takeshi Takahashi
Picture Researcher Patricia Burns
Cover Designer Keith Trego

First Printing

1 3 5 7 9 8 6 4 2

The Chelsea House World Wide Web address is
http://www.chelseahouse.com

Library of Congress Cataloging-in-Publication Data

Peacock, Nancy.
Great prosecutions / Nancy Peacock.
  p. cm. — (Crime, justice, and punishment)
Includes bibliographical references and index.

ISBN 0-7910-4292-8 (alk. paper)

1. Trials—Juvenile literature. [1. Trials.] I. Title.
II. Series.

K540 .P43 2001
345'07—dc21

                              2001028677

Contents

CRIME, JUSTICE, AND PUNISHMENT

Fears and Fascinations:

An Introduction to
Crime, Justice, and Punishment

By Austin Sarat

We live with crime and images of crime all around us. Crime evokes in most of us a deep aversion, a feeling of profound vulnerability, but it also evokes an equally deep fascination. Today, in major American cities the fear of crime is a major fact of life, some would say a disproportionate response to the realities of crime. Yet the fear of crime is real, palpable in the quickened steps and furtive glances of people walking down darkened streets. At the same time, we eagerly follow crime stories on television and in movies. We watch with a "who done it" curiosity, eager to see the illicit deed done, the investigation undertaken, the miscreant brought to justice and given his just deserts. On the streets the presence of crime is a reminder of our own vulnerability and the precariousness of our taken-for-granted rights and freedoms. On television and in the movies the crime story gives us a chance to probe our own darker motives, to ask "Is there a criminal within?" as well as to feel the collective satisfaction of seeing justice done.

Fear and fascination, these two poles of our engagement with crime, are, of course, only part of the story. Crime is, after all, a major social and legal problem, not just an issue of our individual psychology. Politicians today use our fear of, and fascination with, crime for political advantage. How we respond to crime, as well as to the political uses of the crime issue, tells us a lot about who we are as a people as well as what we value and what we tolerate. Is our response compassionate or severe? Do we seek to understand or to punish, to enact an angry vengeance or to rehabilitate and welcome the criminal back into our midst? The CRIME, JUSTICE, AND PUNISHMENT series is designed to explore these themes, to ask why we are fearful and fascinated, to probe the meanings and motivations of crimes and criminals and of our responses to them, and, finally, to ask what we can learn about ourselves and the society in which we live by examining our responses to crime.

Crime is always a challenge to the prevailing normative order and a test of the values and commitments of law-abiding people. It is sometimes a Raskolnikov-like act of defiance, an assertion of the unwillingness of some to live according to the rules of conduct laid out by organized society. In this sense, crime marks the limits of the law and reminds us of law's all-too-regular failures. Yet sometimes there is more desperation than defiance in criminal acts; sometimes they signal a deep pathology or need in the criminal. To confront crime is thus also to come face-to-face with the reality of social difference, of class privilege and extreme deprivation, of race and racism, of children neglected, abandoned, or abused whose response is to enact on others what they have experienced themselves. And occasionally crime, or what is labeled a criminal act, represents a call for justice, an appeal to a higher moral order against the inadequacies of existing law.

Figuring out the meaning of crime and the motivations of criminals and whether crime arises from defiance, desperation, or the appeal for justice is never an easy task. The motivations and meanings of crime are as varied as are the persons who engage in criminal conduct. They are as mysterious as any of the mysteries of the human soul. Yet the desire to know the secrets of crime and the criminal is a strong one, for in that knowledge may lie one step on the road to protection, if not an assurance of one's own personal safety. Nonetheless, as strong as that desire may be, there is no available technology that can allow us to know the whys of crime with much confidence, let alone a scientific certainty. We can, however, capture something about crime by studying the defiance, desperation, and quest for justice that may be associated with it. Books in the CRIME, JUSTICE, AND PUNISHMENT series will take up that challenge. They tell stories of crime and criminals, some famous, most not, some glamorous and exciting, most mundane and commonplace.

This series will, in addition, take a sober look at American criminal justice, at the procedures through which we investigate crimes and identify criminals, at the institutions in which innocence or guilt is determined. In these procedures and institutions we confront the thrill of the chase as well as the challenge of protecting the rights of those who defy our laws. It is through the efficiency and dedication of law enforcement that we might capture the criminal; it is in the rare instances of their corruption or brutality that we feel perhaps our deepest betrayal. Police, prosecutors, defense lawyers, judges, and jurors administer criminal justice and in their daily actions give substance to the guarantees of the Bill of Rights. What is an adversarial system of justice? How does it work? Why do we have it? Books in the CRIME, JUSTICE, AND PUNISHMENT series will examine the thrill of the chase as we seek to capture the criminal. They will also reveal the drama and majesty of the criminal trial as well as the day-to-day reality of a criminal justice system in which trials are the exception and negotiated pleas of guilty are the rule.

When the trial is over or the plea has been entered, when we have separated the innocent from the guilty, the moment of punishment has arrived. The injunction to punish the guilty, to respond to pain inflicted by inflicting pain, is as old as civilization itself. "An eye for an eye and a tooth for a tooth" is a biblical reminder that punishment must measure pain for pain. But our response to the criminal must be better than and different from the crime itself. The biblical admonition, along with the constitutional prohibition of "cruel and unusual punishment," signals that we seek to punish justly and to be just not only in the determination of who can and should be punished, but in how we punish as well. But neither reminder tells us what to do with the wrongdoer. Do we rape the rapist, or burn the home of the arsonist? Surely justice and decency say no. But, if not, then how can and should we punish? In a world in which punishment is neither identical to the crime nor an automatic response to it, choices must be made and we must make them. Books in the CRIME, JUSTICE, AND PUNISHMENT series will examine those choices and the practices, and politics, of punishment. How do we punish and why do we punish as we do? What can we learn about the rationality and appropriateness of today's responses to crime by examining our past and its responses? What works? Is there, and can there be, a just measure of pain?

CRIME, JUSTICE, AND PUNISHMENT brings together books on some of the great themes of human social life. The books in this series capture our fear and fascination with crime and examine our responses to it. They remind us of the deadly seriousness of these subjects. They bring together themes in law, literature, and popular culture to challenge us to think again, to think anew, about subjects that go to the heart of who we are and how we can and will live together.

*   *   *   *   *

The power of the state to bring charges of crime and wrongdoing is one of its most awesome and dread-inspiring. Because prosecution for a violation of the law is never mandatory, those who are charged with the responsibility of deciding who to charge with what must use their discretion wisely. Generally prosecution is a relatively low visibility activity, seldom much noted except by those against whom it is directed. But because prosecution is both a discretionary function and a very important exercise of governmental power, it is sometimes very controversial. Moreover, where the evil against which a prosecution is directed is great, the work of bringing perpetrators to justice may be of monumental importance. It is in these instances that we may see what Nancy Peacock calls "great prosecutions."

This book provides an in-depth examination of five cases in which prosecutors encountered unusually difficult and complex challenges in the effort to bring evil-doers to justice. From the case against Al Capone to Nuremberg and the prosecution of Charles Manson, it brings us close to the world in which justice and punishment are meted out. In each case, Peacock provides a gripping account of the work that prosecutors do. In each case, she adds greatly to our understanding of the when, why, and how of prosecution. *Great Prosecutions* shows how prosecutors turn abstract commitments to order, security, and justice into real-life institutional commitments.

Hermann Göring on the witness stand at Nuremberg. The landmark prosecution of 21 Nazi officials after World War II established the precedent that a nation's political and military leaders could be held accountable for crimes committed during wartime.

The goal of the legal system is a lofty one: justice. Justice can be a somewhat abstract concept, involving ideals such as fairness, impartiality, and proportionality. But when we boil it down, what justice means to most of us—in the criminal justice arena at least—is simply this: that the innocent are acquitted and the guilty convicted and appropriately punished.

These outcomes are by no means inevitable. Sometimes innocent people are wrongly arrested and convicted. And sometimes guilty people escape punishment.

Various factors explain why everyone who is guilty doesn't answer for his or her crimes. First of all, many crimes go undetected or unsolved by the police. Second, even when authorities know who committed a crime, they need enough evidence—gathered in accordance with strict rules—to make an arrest. Finally, there is the matter of convincing jurors of the defendant's guilt, a vital responsibility that falls to prosecutors. To help prevent the innocent from being convicted wrongly, the American justice system requires the prosecution to prove, beyond a reasonable doubt, the defendant's guilt. A defendant is under no such burden to prove his or her innocence. American criminal trials are also adversarial proceedings, which means that the prosecutor's version of events and interpretation of the evidence will be probed and dissected by defense attorneys. Weaknesses that emerge in the prosecution's argument are likely to produce reasonable doubt among jurors, and hence an acquittal for the defendant. Even when evidence of guilt is fairly strong, a particularly skillful defense lawyer can sometimes win acquittal for his or her client. The result is that sometimes criminals—even those who have committed violent and heinous crimes—go free.

This book examines five cases in which criminals may well have gone free but for a great prosecution. What constitutes such a prosecution? First of all, since justice is the ultimate goal of the legal process, it goes without saying that the defendant in a great prosecution must, in fact, be guilty. In addition, the prosecutor must obtain the conviction while staying within the rules. Using improper means to win a conviction—even when the defendant *is* guilty—is never acceptable. Although it may appear to serve justice in the particular case, such conduct can have a corrosive effect on the entire legal system.

Great prosecutions also necessarily involve great evil. No matter how clever the prosecutorial strategy, no matter how dogged the prosecutor, no one would consider a petty-theft conviction a great prosecution. The damage done by that sort of crime—to the individual victimized and to society as a whole—is relatively minor. The cases in this book, by contrast, involve heinous offenses: murder, serial rape, and one of the 20th century's signature horrors, crimes against humanity. Crimes like these cry out for punishment, and a failure to bring the perpetrators to justice presents a grave moral (and sometimes physical) danger to society and its citizens.

Yet for various reasons, the cases discussed in this book presented uncommonly difficult obstacles for the prosecutors. And that is another element that makes them great prosecutions. A cut-and-dried case, even if it involves a serious crime, wouldn't constitute a great prosecution. In these cases, however, the prosecutors had to go to extraordinary lengths to obtain a conviction. In two of the cases—the prosecutions of organized-crime boss Al Capone and of the leaders of Nazi Germany—prosecutors used legal strategies that had never before been attempted.

In the 1920s, Capone was Chicago's most powerful mobster, and his varied criminal enterprises included illegal gambling, bootlegging (alcohol smuggling), and prostitution. He also earned a reputation for unparalleled ruthlessness, even among his criminal rivals. Capone seemed to revel in lethal violence, ordering— and sometimes personally carrying out—dozens of murders. Yet authorities never seemed to have enough evidence to bring him to justice for these crimes. Finally, a novel solution was devised: if the organized-crime boss couldn't be put away for illegal gambling, liquor law violations, prostitution, or murder, why not prosecute him for failing to pay federal income taxes on the profits he made from his criminal empire? Many newspapers of the day ridiculed this approach, but ultimately it brought down the nation's most infamous gangster. Today the use of tax evasion charges is an accepted strategy for breaking up criminal organizations.

During World War II, the leaders of Nazi Germany planned and ordered some of the most reprehensible acts in recorded history. The Nazis attempted to eliminate Europe's entire Jewish population—along with other groups they considered undesirable—through torture, starvation, forced labor, and mass executions. They also ordered the execution of many innocent civilians in conquered lands in retaliation for attacks on German soldiers, and they directed that certain prisoners of war be shot. By May 1945, the German nation had been militarily defeated. But, the victorious Allies wondered, shouldn't Germany's leaders—who had not only started the war but also directed the appalling way it was carried out—answer personally for their actions? Though prosecuting a nation's leadership for crimes committed during wartime was uncharted territory in international law, the Allies convened a military tribunal in the German city of Nuremberg and put 21 top Nazis on trial. The landmark prosecution established that, like the soldiers who carried out illegal orders on the battlefield, the leaders who gave those orders could be held accountable. Currently, international tribunals are prosecuting crimes against humanity stemming from recent conflicts in Europe and Africa.

In two other cases examined in this book—the trial of the Manson "Family" for a series of seven gruesome murders over an August weekend in 1969, and the trial of Byron De La Beckwith for the slaying of civil rights leader Medgar Evers in 1963—prosecutors may not have broken new legal ground, but they did carry out their duties with uncommon tenacity and skill. In the Manson case, prosecutor Vincent Bugliosi had to sift through a tangle of evidence, much of it mishandled by the Los Angeles Police Department; indeed, Bugliosi himself took a prominent role in gathering evidence, a function normally handled by police. In the courtroom, the prosecutor faced a formidable challenge as well: proving that the Family's leader, Charles Manson—who didn't actually commit the murders in question and wasn't even present when they occurred—controlled his young followers enough to make them kill for him, but that those followers had carried out Manson's wishes of their own free will.

By 1994, when prosecutor Bobby DeLaughter was ready to try Beckwith, the murder of Medgar Evers was more than three decades old. Two trials in the racially charged Mississippi of the mid-1960s had resulted in two hung juries, and now much of the original evidence was lost. Many Mississippians even suggested that the case shouldn't go forward, because there was no point in opening old wounds from the state's troubled past. But, mindful of the Evers family's lack of closure and the affront to justice constituted by the unsolved murder, DeLaughter persisted. He cleverly reconstructed the lost evidence and doggedly sought out new evidence, ultimately bringing Beckwith to justice for his 31-year-old crime.

In the final case in this book, farsighted prosecutors turned to cutting-edge science to win conviction of a brutal serial rapist. DNA fingerprinting, now a mainstay of physical evidence, had never before been used in an American criminal trial. By learning about the complicated forensic technique, applying it to the evidence in their case, and explaining it in terms jurors could understand, the prosecutors put a dangerous criminal behind bars for a long time. Like the others who argued the cases discussed in this book, they constructed a great prosecution.

Bringing Down Public Enemy Number One

The third decade of the 20th century was nicknamed the Roaring Twenties for good reason. It was a time of prosperity and optimism, a time when the booming stock market made investors rich—and when many Americans were willing to spend as never before on the pursuit of fun and recreation. The Eighteenth Amendment, ratified in 1919, outlawed the manufacture, transport, and sale of alcoholic beverages within the United States, thus ushering in the era of Prohibition. But the ranks of American drinkers didn't markedly decrease. Demand for alcohol remained high among those who had formerly been in the habit of taking a drink, and many others were drawn to the illegal bars called speakeasies by the excitement of breaking the law.

One figure who seemed to embody the giddy mood of the Roaring Twenties—and whose meteoric rise coincided with Prohibition—was an Italian-American named Alphonse Capone. Nicknamed Scarface because

Al Capone seemed to embody the giddy and optimistic mood of the Roaring Twenties. But behind the colorful public image lurked a ruthless criminal.

of a cheek-to-chin scar he bore on the left side of his face, Al Capone seemed to do everything in a big way. He built a lavish estate on Palm Island, Florida. One Christmas he reportedly spent $100,000 on presents for friends and family. And when the Great Depression threw millions of Americans out of work in the early 1930s, he opened a soup kitchen that served three meals a day to the hungry in his adopted city of Chicago. One Thanksgiving he fed 5,000 men, women, and children a beef stew dinner. Capone's extravagance and apparent generosity earned him celebrity status along with the gratitude of many Chicagoans.

But there was a darker side to Al Capone that people seemed all too ready to ignore. Capone ran a multimillion-dollar criminal empire built not only on bootlegging (the illegal manufacture and smuggling of alcohol), but also on prostitution and illegal gambling. And he managed that empire ruthlessly, murdering anyone who stood in his way.

The son of Italian immigrants, Capone grew up in Brooklyn, New York, where he became a member of the notorious Five Points criminal gang as a teenager. In 1919, when a Five Points alumnus named Johnny Torrio asked Capone to join his organization in Chicago, Capone agreed. He soon became Torrio's right-hand man, largely because of his propensity for lethal violence.

With the coming of Prohibition, Torrio sensed an opportunity to make vast sums of money in bootlegging. To obtain a bigger share of the profits, he sought to unify some of Chicago's smaller gangs under his leadership. Not every gang leader wanted to serve Johnny Torrio, however. Capone convinced many skeptical hoodlums by orchestrating—and sometimes personally carrying out—beatings and murders of Torrio's rivals.

Competition between Torrio's gang and the equally powerful gang of Charles Dion O'Bannion erupted into a full-scale war, and the streets of Chicago became a

battleground. Deadly gunfights often broke out in broad daylight. Al Capone himself is said to have pioneered the drive-by shooting.

In 1924 three Torrio men murdered O'Bannion, but that wasn't the end of the fighting. George "Bugs" Moran assumed control of the O'Bannion gang, and in 1925 his gunmen critically wounded Johnny Torrio, spurring the crime boss to retire. Torrio left his gang in the hands of Al Capone.

Capone continued the war with the O'Bannion gang while consolidating his hold on Chicago's criminal rackets. His bootlegging, gambling, and prostitution businesses would generate annual revenues estimated at more than $100 million, and Capone's role in scores of murders was an open secret. Yet year after year, he conducted his illegal enterprises largely free from interference by the police and immune from prosecution for his

Capone made a great show of helping the less fortunate in his adopted hometown of Chicago. Pictured here is his soup kitchen for the unemployed on South State Street.

many crimes. The explanation was simple: Capone paid bribes to police and politicians in Chicago, and in return they either left him alone or in some cases even protected his criminal activities. Chicago's mayor, William "Big Bill" Thompson, was on Capone's payroll, as were many city aldermen. And Chicago's chief of police observed, "Sixty percent of my policemen are in the bootleg business." Cops and government officials who persisted in going after Capone were beaten up or murdered.

Still, a few private citizens wanted to end Capone's reign of terror. A group of seven wealthy businessmen formed what they called the Chicago Crime Commission. Commission member Charles G. Dawes, a Chicago banker and politician, had served in the federal government as comptroller of the currency under President William McKinley. Between 1925 and 1929, Dawes was the vice president of the United States under President Calvin Coolidge. Dawes pressed Coolidge for federal help with Chicago's crime problems. In 1926, he took the case to a U.S. Senate committee, but the senators responded that it was not within the jurisdiction of the federal government to suggest solutions for local problems. When a young assistant state's attorney was murdered by the Capone organization, however, opinions began to change.

Another group that tried to stop Al Capone was called the Secret Six. Its members, prominent businessmen who kept their role in the group secret to avoid retaliation, financed the activities of a squad of nine law enforcement agents, led by a Prohibition enforcement officer named Eliot Ness.

Years later, Ness would claim that he and his squad—which he dubbed the Untouchables because they couldn't be bribed by the gangsters—had brought Capone down. In truth, though Ness's persistent raids had certainly been an annoyance for Capone, the real credit for putting Chicago's most infamous crime boss

Aerial view of Capone's Palm Island, Florida, estate. The gangster's lavish lifestyle betrayed his vast wealth and became evidence in the government's tax evasion case.

behind bars belonged to a much more unlikely group: the Internal Revenue Service, or IRS. The IRS is the government agency charged with collecting income tax for the federal government.

Al Capone clearly had a lot of money. His villa on Palm Island, Florida, was evidence of that. But Capone had never paid any federal income tax. If his income could be documented, he might be prosecuted on the federal charge of income tax evasion.

But this was no easy task, as IRS agent Frank Wilson discovered when he moved to Chicago in 1928 and, along with other agents under the direction of Elmer Irey, the chief of the IRS's Enforcement Branch, began a three-year investigation of Capone's finances. Wilson and the other investigators found that Capone was very careful never to sign checks or leave any other

A crowd watches as police remove bodies from Bugs Moran's headquarters, February 14, 1929. The savagery of the St. Valentine's Day Massacre, which Capone ordered, spurred government officials to redouble their efforts to put the gangster behind bars.

written evidence of his income. Even the estate on Palm Island didn't prove that the gangster was concealing money: it had been purchased by a friend and months later deeded to Capone's wife, Mae.

The investigation took on increased urgency after February 14, 1929. On that day Capone gunmen carried out one of the most infamous attacks in the annals of American crime: the St. Valentine's Day Massacre. Capone had decided to eliminate his nemesis Bugs Moran and the remnants of the O'Bannion gang once and for all. As he lolled around Palm Island establishing an alibi, his men laid a trap in Chicago. Moran was told that a truckload of whiskey had been stolen from Capone's distilleries and was for sale at a bargain price. The truck was to be brought to Moran's headquarters at a garage the next morning.

On the 14th, Capone assassins disguised as police

officers pulled up in front of Moran's garage in a car with the markings of the Chicago Police Department. The men present in the garage—six gang members and a friend—assumed that the police were conducting a routine raid. As ordered, they lined up against a wall. The four killers then pulled out submachine guns and opened fire, riddling the victims with bullets. All seven men were killed. Moran escaped death only because he was late in arriving to inspect the phony shipment of stolen whiskey.

When real police officers, along with newspaper reporters and photographers, surveyed the scene in the garage, they were shocked at the brutality of the killings. After walking through the crime scene, one reporter made a grisly joke: he had more brains on his shoes than in his head.

There seemed to be no doubt who was behind the slaughter. "Only Capone kills like that," a shaken Bugs Moran told reporters.

Reports of the carnage outraged Chicagoans who had previously treated Al Capone as a celebrity. More important, the St. Valentine's Day Massacre outraged powerful figures in Washington. Robert McCormick, publisher of the *Chicago Tribune* newspaper and a member of the Chicago Crime Commission, traveled to Washington to meet with the new president, Herbert Hoover. McCormick argued that only the federal government was big enough to stop Capone and that the only likely conviction could come from tax evasion. President Hoover, outraged at Capone's lawlessness, told his secretary of the treasury that he wanted to see Capone in jail. Within days Capone was served a subpoena in Florida to appear before a federal grand jury in Chicago.

Accustomed to manipulating the justice system, Capone had his doctor in Miami send word that the gangster was confined to his bed with influenza and pleurisy and could not appear before the grand jury. But

In a test case that didn't bode well for his younger brother, Ralph Capone (pictured here) was convicted of federal income tax evasion.

Capone's arrogance merely angered federal officials, including FBI director J. Edgar Hoover.

Director Hoover sent FBI agents to Florida to document Capone's movements. They found that rather than being confined to his bed, Capone was going out in public, prompting the federal judge who had issued the subpoena to charge the mobster with contempt of court. Eventually Capone returned to Chicago, probably believing that the police wanted to question him about the St. Valentine's Day Massacre, a crime for which he thought he had an airtight alibi. Testifying before a grand jury, however, Capone admitted that he might have neglected to pay his income tax.

Shortly afterward Capone attended a national meeting of crime bosses in Atlantic City, New Jersey. The other gangsters were furious at Capone's St. Valentine's Day Massacre, which they believed would inevitably lead to a law enforcement crackdown on all organized crime. By the end of the conference, Capone had been persuaded that he would need to serve some time in prison to take the heat off America's mobsters. He arranged to have himself arrested in Philadelphia for carrying a concealed weapon.

Capone was hastily given a one-year sentence, which he began serving in a comfortable jail cell with carpets, plush furniture, and various other amenities. He even received two months off his sentence for good behavior. The warden couldn't say enough about Capone's generosity and arranged for him to be secretly released a day early so the newspapers wouldn't be able to photograph the ex-inmate.

As soon as he was released, Capone returned to Chicago. Although he may have believed that the token jail term would end his troubles with the law, he was quite wrong. In fact, while Capone was away serving his sentence, the government had been busy. Three weeks after the gangster returned to Chicago, his older brother Ralph went on trial for tax evasion. U.S. Attorney George E. Q. Johnson was using Ralph Capone's tax evasion trial as a test case. The trial lasted only two weeks, enough time for the prosecutors to present their carefully researched evidence. The jury returned guilty verdicts on all counts, which didn't bode well for Ralph Capone's famous brother.

Then Frank Loesch, the head of the Chicago Crime Commission, struck another blow against Al Capone by creating a list of "public enemies" and naming him "Public Enemy Number One." In fact, the top five public enemies on Loesch's list were men in the Capone organization. It drew national attention to Capone and worked to dispel the image he tried to cultivate of a modern-day Robin Hood.

Still, Frank Wilson wasn't having an easy time building a tax evasion case against Al Capone. One colleague told him he would have less difficulty "hanging a foreclosure sign on the moon." Then an undercover agent told Wilson that Capone's men were planning to kill him. Instead of scaring him off, this news gave Wilson more resolve to put Public Enemy Number One in jail.

Wilson finally got his break by looking at an accounting ledger that had been in the IRS's possession for five years. Reading the ledger, Wilson realized that he was holding the books of a multimillion-dollar organization. And that organization was providing an income directly to Al Capone. Wilson found the cashier who had kept the ledger and demanded that he talk. But the cashier was more afraid of Capone than of anything the government could do to him.

However, there was something the cashier feared even more than Capone, as Wilson found out from an informant. The cashier, it seemed, was repulsed by and deathly afraid of insects and vermin of all kinds.

Wilson had the cashier arrested and placed in an insect-infested jail cell. He told the man he would be released when he was willing to talk. After five days in his own private hell, the cashier agreed to cooperate. He was brought before a special grand jury that had secretly been convened in the middle of the night.

There the cashier described how he had converted the profits from Capone's gambling houses into cashier's checks and forwarded them to Capone. Finally the federal government had a star witness.

In the meantime, Wilson had located an accountant in the Capone organization. When Capone learned that the accountant had been questioned by the government, he ordered the man killed. This ruthlessness backfired. Instead of silencing him, Capone had given the accountant no choice but to cooperate with the government.

Today witnesses whose lives are threatened can be hidden in the Federal Witness Protection Program. But back then no such program existed. So Wilson persuaded the Secret Six to pay for an extended trip to South America—complete with bodyguards—for the cashier, until Capone's trial date arrived. The accountant was packed off to a remote location in Oregon.

On June 5, 1931, Capone was indicted on 22 counts of tax evasion. The government had been able to find earnings from 1924 to 1929 that totaled more than $1 million. Even though that was only a fraction of Capone's real income, it was enough to prove that he owed the government $215,080 in back taxes.

If a tax evasion prosecution sounds like a novel way to attempt to put a gangster behind bars, in the 1920s it certainly was. First of all, most people at that time didn't have checking accounts. Being able to prove

income and expenses wasn't something the average person needed to be concerned about. Second, only 7 percent of all U.S. citizens even made enough money to be required to pay income tax. The forms were complicated, and the few people who were required to file used a lawyer or an accountant. And third, employers didn't withhold taxes from an employee's paycheck, as they do today.

Capone was relaxed and smiling as his trial for tax evasion got under way. Perhaps that was because his organization could pretty much guarantee an acquittal. Jury selection in those days was much different than it is today. Today the names of jurors aren't publicly revealed before a trial. In Capone's time newspapers published a list of the jurors' names, addresses, and occupations. In previous legal proceedings Capone's organization had been very effective in bribing and threatening jury members, as well as presiding judges.

But Capone hadn't counted on the shrewdness of Judge James H. Wilkerson, the magistrate who had earlier found him in contempt of court for failing to

Capone and his lawyers exude confidence before the start of the gangster's tax evasion trial. Their relaxed attitude is understandable: in previous legal proceedings, Capone had always prevailed—often through bribery, witness intimidation, and jury tampering.

respond to the grand jury summons. When Wilkerson, instead of the judge Capone was expecting, entered the courtroom, the gangster lost his relaxed smile.

Wilkerson had another surprise in store for Capone. Right before the proceedings began, Wilkerson sent the jurors to another judge's courtroom. The jurors from that courtroom, in turn, filed into Wilkerson's courtroom. Without knowing their identities, Capone's men had no way to bribe or intimidate these jurors, who would be sequestered for the duration of the trial. As the realization of what was happening sank in, Capone's face froze in a tight grimace.

Although Capone's attorneys were the best money could buy, they seemed unprepared for the aggressive way in which the prosecutors went about proving their case. Tax evasion was a new category of crime, and Capone's lawyers missed several opportunities to exclude damaging evidence from the trial.

The year before, Capone had hired a Miami lawyer named Lawrence Mattingly to help with his tax problems. In his correspondence with Capone, Mattingly had taken pains not to make incriminating statements, while urging his client to pay the taxes. But those same letters served as evidence that Capone knew he owed back taxes and had not paid them.

Later Mattingly had gone to the IRS's Chicago office with a tax letter he hoped would satisfy the agency. But the letter was filled with legal mumbo jumbo meant to obscure Capone's actual income: "During the years 1926 to 1929, inclusive, he was the recipient of considerable sums of money, title of which vested in him by right of possession only." Capone's lawyers objected to admitting the letter as evidence. Wilkerson overruled them, allowing it to be read into the record.

Prosecution witnesses included a Florida state's attorney who testified that Capone had admitted his chief occupation was gambling. Another witness was

Parker Henderson, whose name Capone had put on the deed of his mansion in Florida. Henderson claimed he'd put his name on the deed to help Capone "avoid publicity." But real-estate records showed that several months later Henderson had quietly changed the name on the house's deed to that of Capone's wife.

The prosecutors produced 50 witnesses, each of whom testified that Capone had spent large sums of money on luxuries and always paid for them in cash. On the rare occasion when Capone was forced to write a check, he had one of his employees sign it and then reimbursed the employee with cash.

At the end of the day, a Friday, the judge adjourned the court and then ordered Capone's bodyguard to be searched. Police found a .38-caliber pistol. Wilkerson was already irritated by the bodyguard's behavior—he had menaced witnesses with threatening looks throughout the day. So the judge had the bodyguard thrown in jail for the weapons violation.

On Monday the prosecutors returned their focus to the lavish spending habits of Al Capone. Clothing salesmen told of thousands of dollars in clothing purchases, right down to the gangster's imported silk underwear.

No piece of evidence was left out. Even Capone's 1930 telephone bill, for $3,061, was introduced over the objections of defense counsel. When Capone's lawyer asked what a 1930 telephone bill had to do with the government's case, which extended only to 1929, the prosecutor replied, "The bill payments show that money was available to pay taxes."

"And they used it to pay telephone bills with," added the judge.

The next day the prosecution called to the stand the cashier who had been hiding in South America. The cashier testified as to how he took the gambling-house profits and bought cashier's checks, which were then turned over to Capone's chauffeur, who gave them

Looking shaken, Capone emerges from federal court. From the outset, prosecutors had Capone's legal team off balance, and ultimately the jury returned guilty verdicts on five counts.

to Capone's financial secretary. A total of 43 cashier's checks were admitted into evidence over the objection of Capone's lawyers. In a final dramatic move, prosecutors showed the jury the signature on one of the checks. It was the signature of Al Capone.

At this point the prosecution, in a development that surprised courtroom observers, rested its case. No one had expected the government's case to be so short, and reporters raced to the phones to call in their stories.

Capone's lawyers, once again caught by surprise, asked Judge Wilkerson for more time to prepare their case. But the judge reminded them that he had sequestered the jury for the duration of the trial. An extension was out of the question.

The defense presented an extremely weak case. Capone's lawyers were not accustomed to trying difficult cases; bribing and intimidating the witnesses, judge, and jury usually made a vigorous legal defense unnecessary.

So his attorneys decided on a flimsy defense strategy. They attempted to show that Capone had lost as much money as he'd made in gambling. His attorneys called independent gambling bookies and Capone employees as witnesses to testify about Capone's staggering gambling losses. Although the bookies could remember the exact amounts of the gambling losses, they couldn't remember any of the other details of the bets, such as the dates or the names of any of the horses on which Capone had wagered.

Had Capone's lawyers been more prepared for a real legal battle, they could have argued that until 1927 profits from illegal activities were not taxable income. Furthermore, they could have argued that Capone had made at least some attempt to pay the taxes by meeting with IRS agents and hiring the tax lawyer.

Instead, the defense's case was capped off by a weak closing argument: that the government was out to get Al Capone simply because he was Al Capone. "Why do they seek conviction on this meager evidence?" Capone's lawyer asked. "Because he is Alphonse Capone. Because he is the mythical Robin Hood you read so much about in all the newspapers. They have no evidence, or what they have produced here discloses only one thing: that the defendant Al Capone is a spendthrift, that he was extravagant."

The jury took 20 ballots and nine hours before reaching its verdict. Although it found Capone not guilty on 17 counts, the jury did find him guilty of three felonies and two misdemeanors. The felonies were for evading taxes on his income in 1925, 1926, and 1927, which the prosecution had shown amounted to at least $645,000—an astronomical amount in 1931. The misdemeanors were for not filing income tax returns in 1928 and 1929.

Capone and his lawyers recognized that the guilty

verdicts would mean heavy fines and some jail time. They were hoping for a 3-year sentence. But Judge Wilkerson came down hard on America's most infamous gangster, sentencing Capone to 11 years, 10 of which were to be served in the federal penitentiary at Leavenworth, Kansas.

Most newspapers cheered the verdict in editorials and front-page headlines. But the *Boston Globe* proclaimed, "It is ludicrous that this underworld gang leader has been led to the doors of the penitentiary at last only through prosecutions on income tax . . . laws."

Capone's lawyers worked desperately to keep their client out of the federal penitentiary. They filed an appeal with the U.S. Circuit Court of Appeals, which upheld the convictions. Next Capone's attorneys petitioned the U.S. Supreme Court.

In the meantime, Capone was sent to the Cook County Jail, where bribery bought him a cushy lifestyle. The warden gave him an oversize cell on the fifth floor that he shared with his bodyguard, who had been given a six-month sentence for perjury and carrying a weapon in the courtroom. The two men enjoyed box-spring mattresses, a radio, and the home cooking of Mae Capone, which was delivered on a regular basis. For Thanksgiving, Capone invited several family members and friends to a banquet served by a butler. Capone also had access to the jail's telegraph system and called his family and business associates on the jail's phone system. Visitors to Capone's cell included Chicago and Illinois officials. But when the U.S. Supreme Court rejected Capone's petition for review of his case, everything changed.

Instead of serving his time in Leavenworth, Capone was sent to the federal prison in Atlanta, an overcrowded institution that was considered the worst in the entire federal system. Years later, Eliot Ness bragged that he had helped escort Capone to the train station.

Although life in the Atlanta prison was grim,

Capone hadn't quite hit bottom. In August 1934, he was transferred to Alcatraz, the new federal facility in San Francisco Bay. He had been selected as one of the 100 most dangerous criminals in the federal system. Rules at Alcatraz were extremely harsh. Guards were forbidden to call prisoners by name but instead used a two-digit number. The convicts weren't permitted to talk to one another.

Capone's mind began to fail. Tests revealed that he was suffering from an advanced case of syphilis, a sexually transmitted disease that in its later stages can affect the brain. At the time, there was no effective treatment. By the end of his sentence, Capone was confined to the prison hospital in a cage for mentally unstable inmates. In November 1939, the man formerly designated Public Enemy Number One was released to his family.

He lived another seven years, but friends and associates judged him completely insane. Shortly after his 48th birthday, Capone suffered a stroke and slipped into a coma. A week later, on January 25, 1947, Al Capone died quietly at his Palm Island villa.

Alcatraz, the maximum-security penitentiary reserved for America's 100 most dangerous federal inmates, was Capone's home between 1934 and 1939.

THE NUREMBERG TRIALS

By 1945 the soldiers of the Allied nations— the United States, Great Britain, France, and the Soviet Union—had witnessed a lot of suffering and death. But during the final weeks of World War II in Europe, as the Allied armies closed in on Nazi Germany, they stumbled upon scenes of horror that shocked even the most battle-hardened veterans. At death camps and concentration camps, unburied corpses lay piled as high as small mountains. Among the tens of thousands of dead walked hollow-eyed survivors so emaciated they looked like living skeletons.

The Nazis, who had ignited World War II by invading Poland in 1939, had also tried to systematically exterminate all of Europe's Jews—who they declared were racially inferior to German "Aryans"— along with Gypsies, homosexuals, the physically handicapped, the mentally retarded, and Communists and dissidents of all kinds. Through torture, starvation, forced labor, and mass executions, the Nazis had killed some 11 million civilians. The sheer scope of the evil staggered the imagination.

By the time of its unconditional surrender in May, Germany had paid a heavy price for its role in World War II. Some 3.5 million German servicemen had been killed in battle, and as many as 300,000 civilians had perished in Allied bombing raids. Much of the country was in ruins, and Allied armies would occupy the entire Fatherland.

If this were like previous wars, the victorious Allies would, perhaps, have compelled Germany to pay reparations, monetary settlements to wronged countries. But that would have ended the matter; there would have been no additional consequences for the German government.

However, the Allies believed that in this case justice demanded more. The Nazi leaders who had initiated the war, and who had devised and directed such policies as the "Final Solution" (the elimination of all Jews), should be held personally accountable for their actions.

There was no precedent for prosecuting an entire government—but then again, history had never witnessed anything that rivaled in scope the evil perpetrated by the Nazis. In the view of the Allies, the Nazi leadership had committed a multitude of war crimes.

War crimes are violations of the rules of warfare, as established by law (through written treaties such as the Geneva Conventions) and by custom. In 1945 the idea of war crimes wasn't new. International law had long recognized that soldiers and their commanders were obliged to conform their behavior to certain norms, even during the heat of battle. The rules governed, for example, how enemy prisoners or wounded must be treated and how civilians in an occupied territory must be treated.

People who broke the rules of war could be prosecuted and punished, by their own country or by an enemy. Because the rules of war were always considered international and binding for everyone, violators could be brought to justice even by a nation that itself had no laws prohibiting the conduct in question.

Over the course of history, individuals had been prosecuted for breaking the rules of war, dating back at least to 1305. In that year an English court convicted and sentenced to death the Scottish rebel leader William Wallace. According to the court, Wallace had indiscriminately killed English citizens, "sparing neither age nor sex, monk nor nun."

But three elements invariably characterized proceedings against people accused of violating the laws of war: the accused were field commanders or ordinary soldiers, as opposed to political leaders; those trying the accused were their enemies; and the trials took place in the midst of war.

The Treaty of Versailles, which officially ended World War I, called for German leaders—including the emperor, Kaiser Wilhelm II—to be tried for war crimes before an international tribunal. In the face of German resistance, however, the international community backed down. Instead of an international tribunal, the German Supreme Court investigated and heard war crimes cases. It acquitted more than 98 percent of the defendants, and the handful who were found guilty received ridiculously light sentences. The kaiser himself was never tried.

After World War II, the Germans couldn't obstruct war crimes trials because this time the Allies occupied their country. Nevertheless, other obstacles existed. One involved the rules under which the defendants would be tried. In British and American criminal procedure, trials are adversarial proceedings. The defense attorney and the prosecutor argue their side of the case in a kind of legal competition. Under this system, the prosecution has the burden of proof—that is, to obtain a conviction, the prosecutor must show with clear and convincing evidence that the defendant is guilty. The judge acts as a referee, presiding over the proceedings to ensure that the rules of law are being followed. But in most of Europe, including France and the Soviet Union, a different system exists. Under the inquisitorial system, an officer of the court presents both the prosecution and the defense. Then the judge or panel of judges decides if the case should be brought to trial. If the case is brought to trial, the defendant is required to prove his or her innocence, and judges take an active role in questioning witnesses.

After long negotiations, the four Allied countries chose to use the adversarial, or British-American, form of trial. The Soviets said that the trials ought to assume the Nazis' guilt and be conducted only to determine the severity of punishment, but the British and Americans wanted trials that determined both the guilt and the punishment. Again, the British and Americans got their wish.

Although the defendants' legal rights would be protected, they would also face certain restrictions. The court would not allow a defendant to base his innocence on the excuse that he was following orders from a superior. The reasoning was simple: In a dictatorship, one person holds power over everyone in the government. In Nazi Germany, that person was Adolf Hitler, and he had committed suicide before the war ended. In addition, the defendants could not use the excuse that the Allies had committed the same crimes. This defense is known in legal circles as *"tu quoque,"* Latin for "so did you."

The Allies created the International Military Tribunal (IMT), an eight-judge panel consisting of one judge and one alternate from each country. Defining the crimes against the Nazis was an enormous project. Ultimately the charges were divided into four counts:

Count One was for conspiracy to wage wars of aggression (undeclared war) in violation of interna-

tional treaties, agreements, or assurances. The conspiracy charge meant that the Allies would hold the Nazis responsible both as individuals and as a group for the crimes.

Count Two was for crimes against peace: planning, preparing, and initiating wars of aggression. Only leaders who formulate policy can be guilty of crimes against peace, as an army's duty is loyalty.

Count Three was for war crimes, including illegal treatment of prisoners of war, civilian ill-treatment or deportation to slave labor, killing hostages, stealing property, and wanton destruction of cities other than for military necessity.

Count Four was for crimes against humanity, including slavery, deportation, murder, inhumane acts against civilians, and persecution on religious, racial, or political grounds.

The eight judges of the International Military Tribunal. Each of the four prosecuting nations—France, Great Britain, the Soviet Union, and the United States—named one lead judge and one alternate.

The defendants' dock. Standing to address the court is Baldur von Schirach, head of the Hitler Youth.

The Americans were given the job of prosecuting all those charged with Count One. The British were responsible for Count Two. The French and Soviets were given Counts Three and Four, which covered crimes committed in eastern and western Europe.

In October 1945, the four chief prosecutors selected 25 high-ranking Nazis to be tried on at least two of the four counts. Unfortunately, neither Hitler—the man probably most responsible for the atrocities—nor two top aides, Heinrich Himmler, head of the dreaded SS elite corps, and Nazi propaganda minister Joseph Goebbels, could be brought to justice. All three had committed suicide in Berlin in April 1945 as Russian troops advanced on the city. Still, many top-level Nazis, including Hermann Göring, commander of the German air force and a top Hitler adviser, had been captured.

On November 20, 1945, the 21 defendants filed into the courtroom of the Palace of Justice in Nuremberg, Germany, and sat in a section called the prisoner's dock. (A 22nd defendant, Hitler's private secretary Martin Bormann, had disappeared in the closing days of the war and was to be tried in absentia.) Some 250 journalists from 23 countries covered the trials. In the days before television, motion-picture cameras were set up to record every moment of the proceedings. These films would be used later in the newsreels that were shown in movie theaters.

All 21 defendants pleaded not guilty. Then Robert Jackson, an associate justice of the United States Supreme Court and the Americans' chief prosecutor at Nuremberg, delivered his opening remarks:

> The privilege of opening the first trial in history for crimes against the peace of the world imposes a grave responsibility. The wrongs which we seek to condemn and punish have been so calculated, so malignant and so devastating, that civilization cannot tolerate their being ignored, because it cannot survive their being repeated. That four great nations, flushed with victory and stung with injury, stay the hands of vengeance and voluntarily submit their captive enemies to the judgment of the law, is one of the most significant tributes that Power has ever paid to Reason.

Jackson acknowledged that the victors had given themselves the right to prosecute and judge the vanquished. But he also pointed out an equally important truth: "If these men are the first war leaders of a defeated nation to be prosecuted in the name of the law, they are also the first to be given the chance to plead for their lives in the name of the law."

In his opening statement Jackson also set up some of the documentary evidence that prosecutors intended

In still photographs and motion pictures, the Allied prosecutors presented graphic images of Nazi atrocities. Here the court is being shown evidence from the concentration camps.

to present to establish the defendants' guilt. "There is no count in the Indictment that cannot be proved by books and records," he declared. "The Germans were always meticulous record keepers. . . . Nor were they without vanity. They arranged frequently to be photographed in action."

To bring the horror of the Nazi regime to life in the courtroom, movies were shown of concentration camps filled with mounds of skeleton-thin corpses. Most of the defendants seemed shocked and sickened by the images.

Testimony from Major General Erwin Lahousen, a survivor of the Nazi counterintelligence group Abwehr, showed that defendants Joachim von Ribbentrop, Hitler's foreign affairs adviser, and Wilhelm Keitel, field marshal of the German armed forces' High Command from 1938 to 1945, were in charge of "political housecleaning," a term for the murdering of all Polish intelligentsia, nobility, clergy, and Jews. Lahousen also told of the Nazis' deliberate withholding of food, shelter, and medical care from Soviet prisoners, causing the death of vast numbers.

When it came time for the British to prosecute Count Two, crimes against peace, chief prosecutor Sir Hartley Shawcross read the testimony of a German construction worker who watched as 5,000 Ukrainian Jews were machine-gunned and dumped in an enormous pit. Further evidence, taken from confiscated German documents, laid out the plans made by the Nazis for the domination of Poland, Denmark, Norway, Belgium, the Netherlands, Greece, Yugoslavia, and the Soviet Union.

Another piece of evidence was the film *The Nazi Plan*. In it many of the defendants were shown carrying out their duties within the Nazi government. Then the Americans presented evidence showing the seven Nazi organizations responsible for war crimes: the Reich Cabinet, the Leadership Corps, the SS, the SD (security service), the SA (storm troopers or brownshirts), the German High Command, and the Gestapo (secret police).

For the prosecution of Counts Three and Four, French survivor Maurice Lampe told of the Nazis' brutal torture and murder of Allied pilots at the Mauthausen camp in Austria. Lampe also described the execution of Soviet officers.

Another Mauthausen witness was photographer François Boix, who worked as a photographer in the death camp. Boix had photos of Nuremberg defendant Albert Speer, Hitler's minister of armaments and munitions, shaking hands with the commandant of Mauthausen. The French prosecutor also read damaging quotes from Speer: "There is nothing to be said against the SS taking drastic steps and putting known slackers in concentration camps. There is no alternative."

The Soviets called a surprise witness: Field Marshal Friedrich Paulus, commander of the German Sixth Army. Paulus identified defendants Keitel, Göring, and Alfred Jodl, chief of staff of the German armed forces' High Command, as active participants in fomenting war against the Soviet Union. The Soviets showed a film of German atrocities that outdid the American film in gore and violence.

Witnesses described how the Germans made soap from human corpses. The testimony included a slide

Field Marshal Friedrich Paulus was a surprise witness for the prosecution. Paulus implicated his countrymen Hermann Göring, Wilhelm Keitel, and Alfred Jodl in fomenting Germany's war of aggression against the Soviet Union.

show of mass executions, baskets full of human heads, and photo after photo of dead bodies and hangings. Witness after witness described the gruesome ways in which people were tortured.

The only defense strategy left to the Nazi defendants was to distance themselves from the well-documented atrocities. As the highest-ranking Nazi, Göring was the first to take the stand. He seemed more interested in being remembered as an important figure than in distancing himself from the power base of Nazism.

"With the dynamic personality of the Führer, unsolicited advice was not in order, and one had to be on very good terms with him," Göring bragged on the witness stand. "That is to say, one had to have great influence, as I had."

Although Göring admitted to having great influence, he insisted he had not known about the genocide of the Jewish people. "These things were kept secret from me," he said. "I might add that, in my opinion, not even the Führer knew the extent of what was going on."

Göring rambled constantly, exasperating American prosecutor Robert Jackson. Jackson tried to force Göring to give yes-or-no answers, but the International Military Tribunal's chief justice permitted Göring wide latitude in order to guarantee him a fair trial. Göring's portion of the trial took 12 days. The other defendants were more succinct.

On the stand, Ribbentrop claimed to know nothing about the persecution of the Jews and the taking of territory from other countries. Keitel admitted that he had done things that were "against the inner voice of my conscience."

Ernst Kaltenbrunner, head of the Reich Central Security Office of the SS, was questioned about his involvement in sending millions of people to death camps. Even though his signature was on thousands of deportation papers, he brazenly denied the charges. "Never once in my whole life did I ever see or sign a single protective custody order," Kaltenbrunner said. Even his attorney remarked that "this statement of yours is not very credible. It is a monstrosity."

Walther Funk had been minister of economics and president of the Reichsbank, Germany's central bank. Though Funk denied any knowledge that his bank had accepted valuables such as gold coins, jewelry, and gold teeth stolen from Jewish victims of the Nazi death camps, movies were shown of the Reichsbank vaults, where bags of these items were stored.

The other banker on trial, Hjalmar Schacht, had been Funk's predecessor as president of the Reichsbank. He admitted that Germany's invasions of the European countries had been acts of aggression and that as president of the national bank, he shared responsibility for the creation of the German army. This acceptance of responsibility weighed in his favor. So did his participation in a plot to assassinate Hitler, for which Schacht was sent to the Dachau concentration camp in 1944.

Navy Grand Admiral Karl Dönitz was charged, among other things, with an order prohibiting the rescue of survivors of enemy ships sunk by submarines. For his defense, Dönitz produced an affidavit from Admiral Chester Nimitz, the U.S. commander of the Pacific Fleet. The affidavit affirmed that U.S. submarines had the same policy toward Japanese warships in the Pacific.

Grand Admiral Erich Raeder, commander in chief of the German navy from 1923 to 1943, was charged with violating the Versailles Treaty by building up the

Robert Jackson, chief prosecutor for the United States, grew frustrated at Hermann Göring's continual digressions during cross-examination. But the court, hoping to ensure a fair trial for the defendant, gave Göring wide latitude.

German navy. By the end of the war, Raeder was 70 years old and knew he would be punished. He confided that he would prefer being shot to serving a prison sentence.

General Alfred Jodl claimed he was one of the few people who dared to confront Hitler with his opinions and tried to soften Hitler's tactics. Bormann's attorney pointed out that his client was dead. Years later, Bormann's charred remains were found in Berlin.

Baldur von Schirach, organizer of the Hitler Youth organization, had been appointed the political district leader of Vienna in 1940. In that post he had sent thousands of Austrian Jews to the death camps. Schirach admitted that he had known about the executions going on in eastern Europe. He told the tribunal, "I alone bear the guilt for having trained our young people . . . for a man who murdered by the millions."

Fritz Sauckel, by contrast, tried to blame defendant Albert Speer for the charges leveled against him:

importing and mistreating 5 million workers from occupied countries.

Speer, trained as an architect, had served as armaments and war production minister under Hitler. Unlike most of the other Nuremberg defendants, Speer unflinchingly accepted responsibility for his efforts to keep the German war machine running smoothly:

> I, as an important member of the leadership of the Reich, share in the total responsibility. Hitler intended, deliberately, to destroy the means of life for his own people if the war were lost. . . . There is one loyalty which everyone must keep; and that is loyalty to one's own people. That duty comes before everything. . . . That Hitler had broken faith with the nation must have been clear to every intelligent member of his entourage, certainly at the latest in January or February 1945.

Artur Seyss-Inquart realized that his role in running the Nazi-occupied Netherlands had sealed his fate. "Whatever I say," he told the tribunal, "my rope is being woven with Dutch hemp."

Franz von Papen, chancellor of Germany in 1932, had paved the way for Hitler to become chancellor in 1933. Papen said he had followed the Nazi party out of his love for Germany.

Hans Fritzsche, who was in charge of Nazi propaganda radio operations, ended his defense with two main points: he claimed ignorance of the Jewish extermination, and he criticized the principles of Nazism. He told the tribunal that "an ideology in the name of which five million people were murdered is a theory which cannot continue to exist."

Final summation from both sides took 19 days. Göring took his last defense opportunity to tell the tribunal that he was innocent, that Hitler had been wrong, and that he, Göring, had done everything out of a sense of patriotism.

On September 30 and October 1, 1946, the

tribunal found only three defendants not guilty: Schacht, Papen, and Fritzsche. The rest of the Nazis were found guilty. Eleven (including the absent Bormann) were sentenced to death by hanging, and the other six received prison sentences ranging from 10 years to life.

Two weeks later, the death sentences were to be carried out. Shortly beforehand, Göring took a capsule of cyanide and poisoned himself. He left a haughty letter for his captors:

> To the Allied Control Council:
>   I would have no objection to being shot. However, I will not facilitate execution of Germany's Reichsmarschall by hanging! For the sake of Germany, I cannot permit this. Moreover, I feel no moral obligation to submit to my enemies' punishment. For this reason, I have chosen to die like the great Hannibal.

The other Nazis were hanged individually. Then their bodies were photographed by a U.S. Army photographer. Afterward the bodies were taken to a crematorium and burned, and the ashes were dumped into a stream that eventually emptied into the Black Sea.

With that final act, the International Military Tribunal disbanded. One of the assistant U.S. prosecutors, Telford Taylor, remained in Nuremberg for more than two years to prosecute an additional 200 Nazi war criminals.

"The most significant thing about Nuremberg is that it happened," wrote Whitney Harris, assistant U.S. prosecutor at Nuremberg. "More important than the punishment of the defendants, or the pronouncements of law, is the simple fact that for the first time in history the judicial process was brought to bear against those who had offended the conscience of humanity by committing acts of military aggression and other crimes."

Critics of the Nuremberg trials objected to the fact that the defendants were tried for breaking laws that

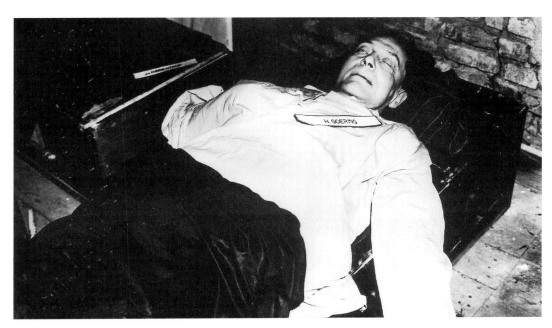

were drafted after the crimes were committed. But the laws involved concepts that were already in place elsewhere in international law. Crimes against civilians and waging undeclared war had been recognized in previous legal codes.

Today people responsible for war crimes and crimes against humanity during recent conflicts in the former Yugoslavia and the African nation of Rwanda have been indicted and tried by an international tribunal at The Hague, Netherlands. The legacy of the Nuremberg trials lives on.

Eleven of the Nuremberg defendants, including Hermann Göring, received death sentences. But Göring cheated the hangman, committing suicide only hours before his scheduled execution.

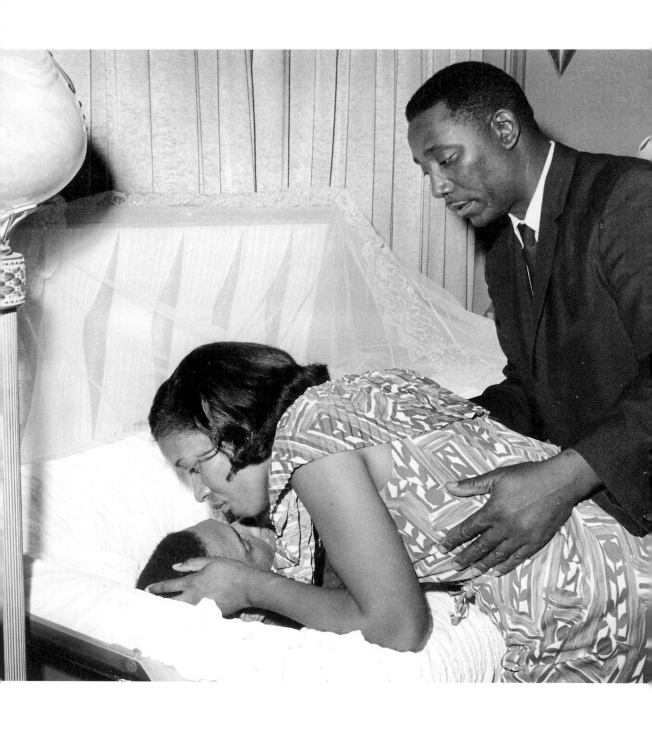

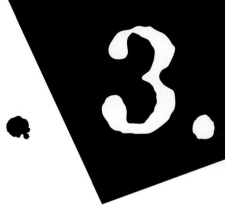

"A LONG TIME COMING": JUSTICE FOR MEDGAR EVERS

Prosecutors know that the chances of bringing a murderer to justice diminish with the passage of time. Memories fade, witnesses disappear or die, evidence gets lost. Yet unlike other crimes, murder carries no statute of limitations: a murder case remains open until it is officially solved. Occasionally, through the tenacity and perseverance of a prosecutor—often combined with a bit of luck—a killer is brought to justice decades after committing the crime.

In January 1994, Bobby DeLaughter prepared to take an old murder case to trial. DeLaughter, the assistant district attorney of Hinds County, Mississippi, had begun digging into the case more than 4 years earlier. At that point the crime was already 26 years old.

It happened in Jackson, Mississippi, after midnight on June 12, 1963. On that hot, sticky night Myrlie Evers was waiting for her husband to come home from work. Medgar Evers had put in another 18-hour day at

Myrlie Evers leans over to kiss the forehead of her murdered husband, civil rights leader Medgar Evers. Behind her is Medgar Evers's brother, Charles.

his job as Mississippi field secretary for the National Association for the Advancement of Colored People (NAACP). Established in 1909, the NAACP is perhaps the best-known civil rights organization in the United States. In 1963, however, many southerners violently opposed the organization's primary goal—to ensure that black Americans enjoyed the same rights as their white counterparts.

For nearly 100 years, African Americans in the South had been second-class citizens. Although slavery had been abolished after the Civil War ended in 1865, many of the defeated Southern states had quickly moved to pass laws designed to maintain the separation of the races and guarantee whites a privileged status. These statutes, called Jim Crow laws, imposed segregation in all public facilities, including restaurants, theaters, hotels, swimming pools, and even public schools. In 1896, in the case of *Plessy v. Ferguson*, the United States Supreme Court upheld the constitutionality of the Jim Crow laws, as long as the accommodations for blacks weren't inferior. Though the facilities for blacks *were* invariably inferior, the "separate but equal" doctrine became the legal standard in the South, where African Americans were prohibited from using any public facility not marked "colored."

In May of 1954, the Supreme Court reversed direction, striking down the concept of separate but equal treatment of the races in the landmark case *Brown v. Board of Education of Topeka*. But the Jim Crow system didn't immediately collapse with the order to integrate public schools.

In Mississippi, as in other states in the South, white supremacists were prepared to go to great lengths to stop integration. They began organizing local Citizens' Councils to preserve the "old order" of a racially divided society. Some members were willing to resort to intimidation, violence, and even murder in the pursuit of their goals. The councils especially believed that

they needed to thwart the efforts of the NAACP, which they claimed was a "Communist front group." Within four years of the *Brown* decision, 80,000 segregationists in Mississippi had joined the Citizens' Councils.

Even the state government embraced white supremacy. In 1956, the state legislature established the Mississippi Sovereignty Commission "to do and perform any and all acts and things deemed necessary and proper to protect the sovereignty of the state of Mississippi . . . from encroachment thereon by the Federal Government or any branch, department or agency thereof; and to resist the usurpation of the rights and powers reserved to this state." This, of course, meant that the state would resist federal orders to integrate. The Sovereignty Commission had an investigative unit run by the former head of the Mississippi Highway Patrol. When an African American met a violent end, particularly if he or she had been a vocal advocate of civil rights, neither the commission's investigative unit nor local law enforcement authorities

Police confront Medgar Evers (center) and NAACP executive secretary Roy Wilkins outside the Woolworth's department store in downtown Jackson, Mississippi, August 1, 1963. Within two weeks Evers would be cut down by an assassin's bullet.

A windowpane with a bullet hole reflects Medgar Evers's car, parked in the driveway where the civil rights leader suffered the fatal wound.

generally attempted to find out what had happened.

All of this made Medgar Evers's position monitoring the progress of civil rights for African Americans in Mississippi one of the most dangerous jobs in the entire state.

Throughout the day of June 11, 1963, Evers called home three separate times, telling Myrlie he loved her and chatting with his three young children. That evening she allowed the children to stay up until their dad got home. When the kids heard the crunch of their dad's tires in the gravel driveway, they shouted, "There's Daddy!" The next thing they heard was a rifle blast.

Darrell and Reena pulled their little brother, Van, to the floor, as their father had taught them to do. But their mother rushed to the front door, screaming. She found Medgar lying facedown in a pool of blood on the driveway. He was holding T-shirts that said "Jim Crow Must Go." Myrlie was hysterical. The three Evers children screamed, "Daddy! Get up!"

Friends loaded Evers into a station wagon and drove toward the University of Mississippi Hospital. But the bullet had torn through his back just below his right shoulder and caused massive internal damage. Evers mumbled and thrashed as he bled to death on the way to the hospital. The driver remembers the civil rights leader's last words: "Turn me loose."

Terrorizing and killing black people was not unusual in Mississippi in 1963. But the murder of Medgar Evers was different. It received *national* attention. *Life* magazine ran photos and an article. This put local and national law enforcement in a bind. Most killings of black people in the South were written off as accidents by the local police and never investigated, much less prosecuted. But the national press was not going to allow this murder to be swept under the rug.

Within a day of the killing, detectives had pieced together the events. The shooter had hidden in a clump of honeysuckle vines under a sweet gum tree in a vacant lot across the street from the Evers home. Paths led away from the spot where the gunman had hidden. Detectives searched the overgrown field. In a hedge next to a ditch, they found a high-powered rifle shoved into some honeysuckle vines. The spent shell was still in place and the gun was fully loaded. When they took the rifle back to police headquarters and dusted it for fingerprints, a nearly complete print was found on the rifle's scope.

Finding the owner of that fingerprint wasn't too difficult. As soon as a picture of the rifle was published in the newspapers, the weapon's original owner realized that it was the gun he had traded to Byron De La Beckwith, a fertilizer salesman and Citizens' Council member from Greenwood, Mississippi. Realizing that the gun would eventually be traced back to him, the original owner gave police Beckwith's name.

The scope of the rifle had its own trail of ownership. After being questioned several times by the FBI, the gun shop owner who had traded it to Beckwith gave agents Beckwith's name. The FBI then matched the fingerprint on the scope with fingerprints from Beckwith's Marine Corps records.

When one of his neighbors informed him that the police had been to his house, Beckwith arranged to turn himself over to police at his lawyer's office. Because no white man had ever been convicted of killing a black man in the state of Mississippi, Beckwith wasn't overly concerned about his future.

Two weeks later, on the day that would have

marked Medgar Evers's 38th birthday, Beckwith was indicted by a grand jury. While various pretrial motions and appeals were being argued, Beckwith stayed in an open jail cell in Rankin County, near a mental hospital where prosecutor Bill Waller wanted him examined. At the Rankin County jail Beckwith was treated like a hero. Local housewives brought him home-cooked meals. The sheriff allowed him to keep a television and some of his gun collection in the cell with him. He could leave his cell and wander around town as long as he was back by dark. Not until the prosecutor finally got the state supreme court to return Beckwith to the Hinds County jail did deputies take away his gun collection.

By 1964, Beckwith's trial was ready to begin. In those days jury selection took a much different form. First of all, women weren't allowed to serve on state juries in Mississippi. Second, of the 100 men chosen as potential jurors, only 7 were black. Of the 7, just 3 were interviewed and none was chosen—a typical outcome. Blacks were never chosen to sit in judgment of a white person. The questions prosecutor Bill Waller asked of potential jurors give a good idea of the racial atmosphere of the time: "Do you think it's a crime to kill a nigger in Mississippi?" "The deceased worked in a way obnoxious and emotionally repulsive to you as a businessman and me as a lawyer—can you put this out of your mind and judge this case like any other case?" "I'm a little upset right now with all these nigras in the courtroom—does that bother you?" After four days a jury of 12 white men was finally impaneled.

Waller's case hinged on establishing that the murder weapon belonged to Beckwith, that the defendant had been in Jackson looking for Medgar Evers's home, and that Beckwith's white Plymouth Valiant had been seen in the neighborhood on the night of the murder. After calling Myrlie Evers, neighbors, and police officers to the stand, the prosecution called a surprise

Byron De La Beckwith (right) confers with his lawyer, Hardy Lott, outside the courtroom. Lott attempted to establish an alibi for his client, presenting witnesses who testified that Beckwith was 90 miles from the crime scene shortly before and after the killing.

witness—Thorn McIntyre, the man who had owned the rifle before Beckwith.

After establishing that McIntyre had traded the rifle to Beckwith, Waller then called an FBI ballistics expert to the stand. The ballistics expert testified that at McIntyre's farm he had found 30 empty cartridge casings that matched the murder weapon. But the bullet that killed Evers had been so mutilated that it couldn't be scientifically matched to the rifle. The telescopic sight on the rifle had come from a gun shop in Beckwith's hometown. On the witness stand, the prosecutor got the owner of that gun shop to identify the scope as the only one of its kind in his store. The next day, the prosecutor produced a fingerprint expert who said he'd found a clear, identifiable fingerprint on the scope. That fingerprint, the expert said, belonged to Beckwith.

Waller also called two cabdrivers, who said that a man they identified as Beckwith had approached them outside the bus station in Jackson and asked if they knew where Medgar Evers lived. The drivers testified that Beckwith had asked about several addresses from a phone book, but that the addresses had all been in white neighborhoods.

Defense attorney Hardy Lott attempted to establish an alibi for his client. Beckwith's hometown of Greenwood is 90 miles south of Jackson. A friend of Beckwith testified that on the night of the killing he had seen the defendant in Greenwood around 11:45 P.M.—45 minutes before Evers was killed. Two Greenwood police officers also testified that they had seen Beckwith at the same gas station at 1:05 A.M., about a half hour after the Evers murder.

The defense then called Beckwith to the stand. He denied shooting Medgar Evers or being in Jackson on the night of the killing. Beckwith testified that his rifle had been stolen, either from his car or from his house, before June 11. Furthermore, he testified that the reason his fingerprint could be found on the scope was that he liked to handle objects in gun shops. As an expert witness for the defense had previously testified, it was impossible to know the age of any fingerprint on the scope.

After a five-day trial, the jury began its deliberations on a Thursday afternoon. By Friday morning, the jury reported that it was hopelessly deadlocked—six for acquittal and six for conviction. Undaunted, Waller announced that he would try the case again.

Jury selection for the second trial didn't begin until two months later. Unbeknownst to the prosecutor, the Mississippi Sovereignty Commission had volunteered to investigate the background of all 300 potential jurors on behalf of the defense lawyers. The commission found one man in the jury pool who was thought to be Jewish. Beckwith's lawyers later struck him from the jury. Once again the defendant got a jury of his peers: 12 Protestant white men.

The second trial was shorter than the first. No transcript of the trial exists because no one ordered a copy and the stenographer's notes have been lost. But newspaper reports give an indication of how the second trial progressed.

One of the cabdrivers who identified Beckwith said he could no longer swear to it, although the cabbie also admitted that he had been threatened and beaten for testifying in the first trial.

Then the defense produced a new witness, who said that he drove a white Valiant just like Beckwith's car. The witness, who was the same height and build as Beckwith, testified that he had gone to the drive-in behind the murder site and had parked his car there on the night Evers was killed.

In his closing argument, Beckwith's lawyer told the jury that his client had been framed, that someone had planted the gun in the bushes. The jury deliberated for two days before becoming deadlocked. This time the jurors were less equally divided, however. Eight deemed Beckwith not guilty; only four wanted to convict.

Prosecutor Bill Waller didn't ask for a third trial because he didn't think he could convict Beckwith without new evidence. The judge set bond, and Beckwith was released that afternoon. Technically he had not been exonerated and still stood accused of the murder. But Beckwith saw it as the end of his legal battles. That night a local hotel treated him and his wife to a free steak dinner. In celebration the Ku Klux Klan burned crosses in almost half the counties in Mississippi.

After the trial, Myrlie Evers left Mississippi and moved to southern California. In March of 1969, a new county prosecutor dropped the murder indictment against Beckwith and refunded his bail bond.

Beckwith had become a hero in the eyes of white supremacists, and he just couldn't walk away from his celebrity. It would eventually become his undoing.

The FBI had infiltrated the Ku Klux Klan after Medgar Evers's death and had monitored Beckwith's activities since his release. In 1970 an informant reported that Beckwith planned to bomb the house of a Jewish leader in New Orleans. Police pulled Beckwith over on the highway to New Orleans. In his car they found a bomb and a map of the intended victim's neighborhood.

Beckwith was arrested and charged with federal and state crimes. At his federal trial in 1974, he told the jury that he didn't know how the bomb or the map had gotten into his car. Miraculously, he was acquitted. But the next year, a Louisiana state jury convicted him, and Beckwith received a five-year sentence. He served three years before being released for good behavior.

Life might have gone on without a hitch for Beckwith. But by the late 1980s, Mississippi had undergone some fundamental changes. In 1987 a black man was elected governor. By the end of the decade, more than 600 African Americans held public office in the state.

In 1989 the *Jackson Clarion-Ledger* reported that the now-defunct Mississippi Sovereignty Commission had investigated the background of the jurors in Byron De La Beckwith's second trial for the murder of Medgar Evers. In the wake of the revelations, the Jackson City Council voted to have the Hinds County district attorney's office look into the matter. Although a grand jury found no evidence of criminal tampering by the Sovereignty Commission, it recommended that the Evers case be reopened.

The job of resurrecting the case fell to assistant prosecutor Bobby DeLaughter. DeLaughter faced a formidable task. Over the years, most of the evidence in

the 25-year-old case had gotten lost. "The DA's file was nowhere to be found," DeLaughter explained. "We did not have the benefit of a trial transcript to know who the witnesses were. None of the evidence had been retained by the court."

Nevertheless, after the assistant prosecutor met with Myrlie Evers, he became, in his words, "a man obsessed." And the widow of Medgar Evers was able to provide a key piece of evidence: a copy of the transcript from the first trial, the only one known to exist. She had kept the transcript locked away for more than 25 years.

Despite the changes in Mississippi's racial climate since the early 1960s, not everyone wanted the district attorney's investigation to go forward. "The easy thing to do," DeLaughter said, "would have been to just leave it alone, because the most frequent thing I was told . . .

After Beckwith's second trial ended in a hung jury, the Ku Klux Klan celebrated by burning crosses in nearly half of Mississippi's counties.

A police expert examines the Evers murder weapon, a .30-caliber deer rifle, June 12, 1963. The rifle, like much of the evidence, would disappear after Beckwith's second trial. In a strange twist, however, the weapon ended up in the possession of prosecutor Bobby DeLaughter's father-in-law.

was 'leave it alone; you're just going to open up an old wound.'" But the prosecutor was spurred on by a sense that justice—for the Evers family and for the people of Mississippi—had never been done. "There are some things," DeLaughter explains, "that not only span races, that not only span people, but span time, as well. It may have been 25 years, but the hurt was still there—the lack of closure, the lack of justice was still there."

DeLaughter continues, "I also considered it a black eye to Mississippi after all those years, and I considered it an opportunity to show that equal justice could be obtained here."

Slowly the investigation began to gain momentum. A police sergeant cleaning out a file cabinet found negatives of the Evers crime scene. An even more amazing coincidence concerned the murder weapon. Fifteen years earlier, when DeLaughter and his wife were newlyweds, his father-in-law had told him that one of the guns in his house was the murder weapon from an old civil rights case. His father-in-law had since died, but DeLaughter called his mother-in-law and discovered that she still had the gun. The serial numbers matched Beckwith's rifle. The murder weapon had fallen into DeLaughter's lap.

While he believed his case against Byron De La Beckwith was coming together, DeLaughter later said, "I always felt like we needed something new, something that [Bill] Waller didn't have. Even if it wasn't necessary legally, I thought a jury psychologically would insist on it."

DeLaughter found something new, and it grew out of an unlikely source: a lawsuit over the 1988 motion picture *Mississippi Burning*. The movie, based on the real-life murder of three civil rights workers in 1964, had angered the Ku Klux Klan. The Klan brought a defamation action against Orion Pictures, the company that had released the film. An attorney friend of DeLaughter's who was representing Orion told the Hinds County prosecutor about an obscure book, out of print for more than 20 years, that he had uncovered. In the book the author, a former FBI informant, described a Klan rally he attended shortly after Byron De La Beckwith's release. At the rally Beckwith, the featured speaker, admitted that he had killed Medgar Evers. DeLaughter tracked down and interviewed the author. He now had what amounted to a confession.

Newspaper reports of the investigation spurred other informants to come forward. "[Beckwith] couldn't resist bragging to people he thought would be impressed with his accomplishment," DeLaughter explained. "What he hadn't counted on was over the years that these people would have a change of heart, that these people would change, unlike him, and they wanted to set things right."

A grand jury that was convened in December 1990 indicted Beckwith again for the murder of Medgar Evers. His new attorneys tried to argue that he had been denied a speedy trial, which is guaranteed in the U.S. Constitution's Bill of Rights. But the judge denied the motion. This set off a series of legal appeals that went all the way to the U.S. Supreme Court. In the fall of 1993, the Court refused to hear Beckwith's lawyers' motion to dismiss.

Jury selection began the following January. This time the jury included eight blacks and four whites. By

1994 there was no need to ask jurors, "Do you think it's a crime to kill a nigger in Mississippi?"

Thirty years had passed since the first trial. But DeLaughter and Hinds County prosecutor Ed Peters somehow had to bring Medgar Evers back to life so the jury would be moved by his death. Their first witness was Myrlie Evers Williams, who had remarried since the murder of her husband.

DeLaughter started by asking about her present life. Then he turned back the clock to the 1950s, when she first met Evers in college.

Next DeLaughter asked her to identify a group of photos. Most were from the crime scene; however, she had never before seen the last photo. Taken shortly before the third trial, it was a photo of her husband's body when his coffin had been opened for a new autopsy. The photo brought tears to Myrlie's eyes; Medgar's body was almost perfectly preserved. The forensic expert who did the autopsy had been amazed at the condition of the body. Evers looked like someone asleep, not dead for 30 years. "This is Medgar in his casket," Myrlie said, her voice cracking.

DeLaughter had the testimony of dead witnesses read into the record. The defense objected, but the judge allowed the testimony. The prosecutor also produced four living witnesses who explained that Beckwith had either admitted he'd killed Medgar Evers or been introduced to them as the man who killed Medgar Evers.

This information was further substantiated by the FBI informant–turned–author, who testified that he had heard Beckwith say at the Klan rally in 1965, "Killing that nigger did me no more physical harm than your wives have to have when they're having a baby for you."

An FBI agent confirmed that the informant had reported this statement in 1965. But the FBI had chosen not to act on it in order to preserve the informant's

Byron De La Beckwith speaks to reporters from the porch of his home in 1990, the year a grand jury indicted him once again for the murder of Medgar Evers.

cover during an ongoing investigation of the White Knights of the Ku Klux Klan.

The third murder trial of Byron De La Beckwith was the top story on CNN's news cycle. After seeing a CNN report, a man living in Chicago called the Hinds County prosecutor's office. Mark Reilly had been a prison guard in Louisiana and knew Beckwith from his three years in prison. Reilly said that Beckwith had bragged about killing Evers. And that wasn't the only information that Beckwith had shared with him. Beckwith had told Reilly that black people were "beasts of the field," like animals. Whites, God's chosen people, were supposed to rule over beasts of the field. If they got out of line, a white could kill beasts of the field and not feel guilty about it. Also, Reilly had heard Beckwith arguing with a black nurse who worked in the prison. Beckwith had shouted, "If I could get rid of an uppity nigger like Medgar Evers, I would have no problem with a no-account nigger like you!"

Myrlie Evers Williams, flanked by her son Darrell and daughter Reena, speaks to the media after the guilty verdict against Byron De La Beckwith.

The defense started by moving for a mistrial. When that was denied, Beckwith's lawyers had the testimony of the dead alibi witnesses read into the record. Then they called several living alibi witnesses.

Beckwith's lawyers asked the judge to rule that their ailing client was incapacitated and couldn't remember the facts of the case. But the judge ruled that Beckwith could read from and refer to the transcript of the first trial. The judge also said that he would not restrict Beckwith's testimony. In the face of this decision, defense lawyers chose not to let their client testify.

Myrlie Evers Williams was disappointed that Beckwith's lawyers kept him off the stand. But another courtroom observer, 73-year-old Rosa Mitchell, was glad not to listen to Beckwith rant and rave. "Now he can't be carrying on like a cobra, spitting out poison at our children," she said. "This poison and hate will end here, with this old man. It ends here, today."

The closing arguments were nearly the reverse of

the arguments of 30 years before. The defense lawyers pleaded with the jury to judge the evidence and not the person accused of the crime. In his closing remarks, prosecutor Ed Peters called Beckwith "a back-shooting, sneaking coward." In reference to the defense lawyers' appeal to consider the evidence over the defendant, Peters replied: "No wonder they don't want you to think about the defendant!"

"All we're asking you people to do is to give the Evers family some justice," Peters continued. "Just justice after 30 years."

After less than a day of deliberations, the jury announced that it had reached a decision. No one was prepared for such a quick verdict. Myrlie, her son Darrell, and her daughter, Reena Evers-Everett, were still at their hotel. They raced to the courthouse and took their seats. Then the jury was called in.

"Have you reached a verdict?" asked the judge.

"Yes," said the jury foreman, handing the judge a piece of paper.

The judge read it silently and handed it to his bailiff. She read it aloud to the packed courtroom: "We find the defendant guilty as charged."

"Yes!" Darrell shouted. Immediately the overflow crowd in the hallway erupted in a cheer.

The judge sentenced Beckwith to life in prison, with a mandatory 10 years before he would be eligible for parole.

Myrlie Evers Williams said she was "deliriously relieved" at the outcome. "It's like taking a deep breath and letting the air out of your lungs very slowly and saying 'it's over' and really meaning it," she explained.

Added Medgar Evers's brother, Charles: "Justice finally came. It was a long time coming, but she's welcome home."

HELTER SKELTER: THE TRIAL OF THE MANSON FAMILY

When Mrs. Winifred Chapman reported for her job as a housekeeper on Saturday morning, August 9, 1969, she noticed a disconnected telephone wire hanging over the gate of her employer's secluded home. As she pushed the button controlling the security gate of the property, located in the exclusive Bel Air suburb of Los Angeles, Mrs. Chapman made a mental note to check the phones in the house. She walked up the drive, unlocked the kitchen door, and picked up the phone. It was disconnected.

Thinking she should tell someone, Mrs. Chapman walked into the dining room. What she saw there stopped her. The floor, the walls, the furniture, the front

On the lawn of a secluded property leased by film director Roman Polanski and his wife, actress Sharon Tate, police detectives and members of the coroner's office examine the body of the couple's friend Abigail Folger. The sheet in the foreground covers the body of Folger's boyfriend, Voytek Frykowski.

step—all were splattered with blood. Through the open front door, out on the lawn, she saw a body.

She ran back through the house, down the driveway, and down the hill, screaming "Murder, death, bodies, blood!" Neighbors called the police.

When three uniformed police officers arrived at the property, the full horror of the murder scene unfolded. Walking up the driveway, they passed a small car with the body of a teenage boy inside. The boy's clothes were soaked with blood. Investigators would soon learn that he had been shot four times.

Officers who proceeded toward the house found the bodies of a man and a woman on the front lawn. They had been stabbed so many times that the police officers described them as looking like mannequins that had been dipped in red paint and thrown on the grass. The male victim had also been shot and beaten severely about the face.

On the front door, someone had written the word *pig* in what appeared to be blood. Inside the house, the police found two more bodies in the living room. A young woman who was obviously pregnant lay on her side. She had been stabbed repeatedly. A rope looped around her neck had been thrown over one of the rafters in the ceiling. The other end of the rope was looped around the neck of a man, whose face was covered by a towel. He was lying on his side with his hands near his head, as though he'd been trying to protect himself. He had been shot and stabbed.

After searching the mansion, the police saw a guest house at the back of the property, past the swimming pool. As they approached the house, a dog began to bark, and they heard someone say, "Shh! Be quiet." The officers surrounded the house and then kicked in the front door. Inside they found a young man, whom they handcuffed and brought outside.

The young man, 19-year-old William Garretson, was the property's caretaker. He kept asking what was happening. The police brought him to the main house and showed him the bodies on the front lawn.

When questioned about the murders, Garretson claimed he hadn't heard or seen anything the previous night. The police didn't believe his story and arrested him. In response to the uniformed officers' call reporting the killings, homicide detectives and forensic evidence specialists began arriving at the crime scene. By this time, reporters were already gathering outside the gate.

Under ordinary circumstances, the gruesome murders would have attracted ample attention from the press. But there was an additional reason for reporters' interest in the case: the house was leased by two Hollywood celebrities, film director Roman Polanski and his wife, actress Sharon Tate.

Polanski was in London finishing a movie, so the police brought his business manager to the mansion to identify the bodies. The pregnant woman was Sharon Tate. The other victims were celebrity hairstylist Jay Sebring, who had formerly been engaged to Tate; Abigail Folger, heiress to the Folger's coffee fortune; and Folger's boyfriend, Voytek Frykowski, a jet-set playboy who was also a friend of Polanski's. The teenage boy in the car was the only victim Polanski's business manager couldn't identify.

In a homicide investigation it's extremely important that the crime scene not be disturbed, to preserve clues and evidence that might prove important. Unfortunately, with scores of policemen, detectives, and forensic specialists swarming all over the Bel Air property, sloppy investigative procedures took a toll on the evidence. A police officer pushed the button to open

Blond and beautiful, Sharon Tate had appeared in TV shows and starred in the film Valley of the Dolls. *Her celebrity ensured that the murders in Bel Air would generate a media frenzy.*

the security gate, thus superimposing his fingerprint on a bloody fingerprint and rendering it useless for identification purposes. Officers stepped in pools of blood outside the house and then tracked blood inside, making it next to impossible to determine whether bloody footprints had been left by the killer or killers. Trunks and pieces of a broken gun grip were moved from their original locations. Forensic specialists failed to collect and test all the blood samples. The loss of this and other evidence would make the case more difficult to solve and, later, to prosecute.

Because nothing appeared to have been stolen from the house or the victims, police quickly ruled out robbery as a possible motive for the killings. And in any event, the murders seemed too savage to have been committed in the course of a robbery. Police found small quantities of cocaine, marijuana, and hashish, along with a few capsules of a drug called MDA. This led them to theorize that the victims had been in the midst of a drug deal or a party when one of the participants had gone temporarily insane and killed everyone. It made as much sense as any other possible motive.

One of the first police officers at the scene had commented to reporters that the murders appeared to have been carried out in a ritualistic fashion. At this point, police weren't releasing many details of the crime, so that officer's statement led to wild speculation in the media. Soon the newspaper headlines spoke of ritual murders and a blood orgy.

The police hoped that Garretson, the caretaker, would be the key to solving the case. The more detectives questioned him, however, the less convinced they became that he was involved—or that he knew anything about the crime. He told police that he had stayed up all night listening to his stereo. His only visitor had been a young man named Steve Parent, whom Garretson said he barely knew. Parent had come to the guest house to try to sell Garretson a clock radio.

But when Garretson said he wasn't interested, his visitor had left.

When police showed him the body in the car, Garretson didn't recognize the victim. A license plate check led to Parent's family, however, and the 18-year-old victim was positively identified.

On Sunday, August 10, William Garretson submitted to a polygraph, or lie detector test. He passed, the polygraph examiner concluding that he was being truthful in denying any role in the Tate murders (as the five killings became known).

Only a few hours later, another set of bizarre slayings was discovered. In the Los Feliz suburb of Los Angeles, the bodies of Leno LaBianca, a grocery-chain owner, and his wife, Rosemary, were found in their home by Rosemary's teenage son and her daughter's boyfriend. Leno had been stabbed to death in the living room. His hands were bound behind his back with a leather thong, and a cord around his neck was attached to a heavy lamp. A carving fork was stuck in his abdomen, and the word *war* had been carved on his stomach. When police removed the bloody pillowcase from his head, they found a kitchen knife sticking in his throat.

In the bedroom, Rosemary LaBianca had been stabbed so many times that police at the crime scene couldn't even count the wounds. Her face, too, was covered by a pillowcase, and a lamp cord had been tied tightly around her neck.

On the refrigerator, in blood, someone had printed "healter skelter," misspelling the first word of the term. On the living room wall, also in blood, were "death to pigs" and "rise."

Almost immediately, the media linked the Tate and LaBianca murders. Yet in spite of the many similarities, the Los Angeles Police Department (LAPD) officially announced that there was no connection between the two cases. LAPD's Tate investigation focused on the

A policeman stands guard in the driveway of the LaBianca residence while other officers look for clues near the door. A day after the Tate killings, Leno and Rosemary LaBianca were savagely murdered inside their home.

drug angle, but no illegal drugs had been found at the LaBianca murder scene.

In the following weeks, with the police giving out little information about the murder investigations, wild rumors, misinformation, and all manner of speculation abounded in the media. The pressure to solve the cases was enormous, but the police, in fact, were making little progress. The authorities didn't know it yet, but they had some of the murderers behind bars on other charges.

On August 16, a week after the Tate-LaBianca murders, the Los Angeles Sheriff's Office (LASO) had raided Spahn's Movie Ranch. The dusty ranch, located in the Simi Hills near Chatsworth, northwest of Los Angeles, had previously served as the set for various Western motion pictures. Now the ranch's 81-year-old owner, George Spahn, made his meager living primarily from city dwellers who came on weekends for horseback riding. But besides Spahn and a handful of his employees, another group had taken up residence on the ranch. Consisting of several dozen young women and men, most in their teens and early twenties, this group might have seemed like just another hippie commune whose members had rejected the values of "the establishment." They took drugs, practiced free love, and called themselves the Family. Their leader was a charismatic 34-year-old named Charles Milles Manson. Many of his followers believed he was Jesus Christ.

Beneath the surface, however, the Manson Family bore little resemblance to the hippies who had dropped out of American society because of its materialism and its involvement in the Vietnam War. Manson, an ex-convict, had spent half his life behind bars, and his Family was involved in criminal activities such as auto theft. That, in fact, was the crime that spurred the August 16 LASO raid.

A few days after the suspects were arrested, however, all had to be released on a technicality: the arrest warrant carried the wrong date. The Family moved to an even more remote spot called the Barker Ranch, which was located in Inyo County on the edge of Death Valley.

In early October, Inyo County authorities raided Barker Ranch and arrested 24 people, charging them with crimes ranging from grand theft to arson. During the raid officers discovered two frightened teenagers

Charles Milles Manson, charismatic leader of "the Family." Some of his followers believed Manson was Jesus Christ.

trying to get away from the Family. The girls had heard that some of the Family had killed a music teacher in Los Angeles named Gary Hinman. One of the teenagers also reported that Family member Susan Atkins had bragged about stabbing a man in the legs.

When detectives questioned Atkins, she admitted that she and Family member Bobby Beausoleil had gone to Hinman's house to take some money they believed he had inherited. When the music teacher wouldn't give them the money, Beausoleil slashed Hinman in the face. The two held the music teacher prisoner for two days, Atkins said, until a struggle occurred during which Beausoleil stabbed Hinman to death. Significantly, Hinman had *not* been stabbed in the legs.

Atkins was taken to the San Dimas police station and booked for suspicion of murder, then transferred to Los Angeles. She hadn't been in the L.A. jail long before she told two inmates all about Gary Hinman's murder. Several days later, she described in detail how she, along with two other women and a man named Charles, had committed the Tate murders. She also confessed that she'd participated in the LaBianca killings.

In November, LAPD detectives interviewed two members of the Straight Satans motorcycle gang. The bikers told police they knew Charles Manson and his Family. Manson had bragged about killing five "pigs" (the number of victims in the Tate case), and while the bikers didn't have any firsthand knowledge of the Tate or LaBianca murders, some of the details they'd heard—such as a message written in blood on the LaBiancas' refrigerator—were tantalizingly similar to evidence found at the crime scenes. Around the same time, detectives interviewed one of the prisoners to whom Susan Atkins had confessed her participation in the Tate, LaBianca, and Hinman killings. From the bikers and this informant, a picture of the murderous Manson cult began to emerge. However, many of the details of the crimes, such as which members of the Family were involved, remained unclear.

On November 18, the Los Angeles district attorney assigned Vincent Bugliosi and Aaron Stovitz to prosecute the Tate-LaBianca case. Stovitz would later be removed for speaking to the press. For Bugliosi the case would become a near obsession: for the better part of the next two years he would work seven days per week—averaging 100-hour workweeks—investigating, interviewing witnesses, and prosecuting the Tate-LaBianca defendants.

At the outset, the prosecution's case looked extremely weak. Susan Atkins's confession to two jailhouse snitches, Manson's ambiguous words about getting "pigs," and the observations and inferences of the Straight Satans bikers weren't nearly enough even to establish what had happened, let alone get convictions. Who besides Atkins had participated in the killings? Where was the gun used at the Tate residence? What was Manson's role? More fundamentally, why had the gruesome murders been committed?

Through a clever interrogation of Leslie Van Houten, detectives pieced together some of the puzzle. The 20-year-old, known within the Manson Family as LuLu, revealed that four Family members had gone to the Tate residence on the night of the murders: Atkins; Patricia Krenwinkel; a woman Van Houten knew only

Charles "Tex" Watson led the killers at the Tate residence. But because Watson fled to Texas and fought extradition, he couldn't be tried with the others.

as Linda, who turned out to be Linda Kasabian; and an unnamed man. Based on a fingerprint found on the front door of the Tate house, police assumed that the man was Charles "Tex" Watson.

On December 1, Edward Davis, chief of the LAPD, called a press conference to announce that his department had solved the Tate case. He informed the more than 200 members of the national and international media who were present that warrants had been issued for Watson, Krenwinkel, and Kasabian. All three, Davis said, had also been involved in the LaBianca murders.

In reality, the chances of convicting these three—or anyone else involved in the murders—were slim. Much of the evidence, such as Susan Atkins's jailhouse confessions, was hearsay and would be inadmissible in court. To build a successful case, prosecutors needed much more, so the district attorney's office decided to offer Atkins a deal. If she testified truthfully about the killings in front of a grand jury, the prosecution wouldn't seek a death penalty, and even if she later failed to testify at the trial, none of her grand jury testimony could be used against her. Atkins agreed to the deal.

Testifying before the grand jury, Atkins revealed that on the night of August 8, Charles Manson had told her, along with Patricia Krenwinkel and Linda Kasabian, to go with Tex Watson and do whatever he said. The four had driven from the Spahn ranch to the Tate residence in a car borrowed from one of the ranch hands. After Watson had cut the telephone wires outside the gate, the four had climbed over the fence surrounding the property. When they saw headlights coming down the driveway, Watson had stopped the car and shot the driver, Steven Parent.

Watson then got into the house through a window, Atkins testified, and let her and Krenwinkel in the front door. Kasabian remained outside and took no part in the violence that followed.

Atkins testified that Voytek Frykowski had been asleep on a couch in the living room. As he awoke, Watson stuck a gun in his face and ordered him to be quiet. Watson then told Atkins and Krenwinkel to search for other people inside the house. They found Abigail Folger in one bedroom, reading; Sharon Tate and Jay Sebring were talking in another bedroom. At knifepoint the intruders herded the three into the living room. Watson told the captives to lie on the floor. When Sebring failed to follow his orders, Watson shot him.

After Atkins tied Frykowski's hands behind his back with a towel, Watson looped one end of a rope around Sebring's neck and threw the other end over a ceiling beam, tying it around the necks of Tate and Folger.

Atkins testified that Watson told her to kill Frykowski, but he managed to free his hands and knock her down. In the struggle that ensued, she said,

Frykowski grabbed her from behind by the hair, and she slashed at him with her knife. He bolted for the door, where Watson caught him, hit him over the head with the butt of the pistol, and stabbed him. Meanwhile, Abigail Folger had managed to get free also and was struggling with Patricia Krenwinkel. Eventually both Folger and Frykowski were killed on the lawn.

Next, Atkins testified, Watson told her to kill Sharon Tate. She couldn't, she claimed, so she held Tate while Watson stabbed her to death. (This contradicted Atkins's earlier statements, during which she admitted to killing Tate herself.)

The following night, Atkins continued, the same four who had been to the Tate residence were joined by Manson and two other Family members: Leslie Van Houten and Steve Grogan. The seven drove around for a while, until Manson got out and entered a house. A short time later, he came out, saying that he had tied up two people inside. Manson ordered Watson, Krenwinkel, and Van Houten to go inside and kill them, then hitchhike back to the ranch. The other four drove away.

On December 8, on the basis of Atkins's testimony, the grand jury returned murder and conspiracy indictments against six defendants: Charles Manson, Charles Watson, Leslie Van Houten, Patricia Krenwinkel, Linda Kasabian, and Susan Atkins.

As the trial date approached, prosecutor Vincent Bugliosi worked feverishly, conducting dozens of interviews and giving LAPD detectives an extensive list of investigative tasks. This was more than was expected of a prosecutor. "Traditionally," Bugliosi wrote in *Helter Skelter,* a book about the Manson case, "the role of the prosecutor has been twofold: to handle the legal aspects of the case; and to present in court the evidence gathered by law-enforcement agencies. I never accepted these limitations. In past cases I always joined in the investigation—going out and interviewing witnesses myself, tracking down and developing new leads, often finding evidence otherwise overlooked."

Even with Bugliosi's extra efforts, the prosecution's case appeared shaky. Many legal observers were, in fact, predicting that the judge would dismiss the charges against all the defendants for lack of evidence. Essentially, the prosecution's case hinged on the testimony of Susan Atkins. But her status as a codefendant of Manson, Krenwinkel, Van Houten, and Kasabian—Watson had fled to Texas and couldn't be tried with the others—presented legal problems. Under the California Supreme Court's 1965 *People v. Aranda* ruling, the prosecution couldn't introduce testimony from one defendant that incriminated codefendants at the same trial. Thus, if Atkins said, for example, "We killed the five people at the Tate house," that statement would be inadmissible in court. However, if she said, "I stabbed Sharon Tate to death," that would be admissible because it didn't implicate any of her codefendants.

The question of how useful Atkins's testimony would ultimately be became a moot point anyway. In early 1970, after a short meeting with Manson, Atkins claimed she had fabricated the whole story. The district attorney's office voided its deal with her, but the already tenuous prosecution case appeared to have collapsed.

Fortunately, Linda Kasabian was willing to testify, and she would make a better witness. Although she had gone on the killing sprees both nights, unlike Atkins she hadn't participated in any of the murders. Plus she was repulsed by what had happened and had run away from the Family two days after the LaBianca killings. The district attorney offered her a deal: after she testified fully and truthfully against all the defendants, she would receive full immunity from prosecution. Kasabian accepted the deal.

As the beginning of the trial loomed, it became clear that Manson still exerted a great deal of control over his three remaining codefendants, all young women between the ages of 20 and 22. Behind the scenes, the 35-year-old ex-con appeared to be directing everyone's defense strategy to serve his own interests. For example, whenever an attorney for one of the women began exploring an insanity defense—which would benefit his client but not Manson—that attorney was dismissed. Manson's women, it seemed, were willing to protect him even if it might mean the death penalty for themselves.

That situation underscored the difficult task facing prosecutors. To obtain a first-degree murder conviction against Manson, who hadn't been present during any of the killings, they had to show that he controlled his codefendants to such an extent that they would do anything he asked—even brutally murder total strangers—and that he had ordered them to carry out the slayings. On the other hand, to obtain first-degree murder convictions against Atkins, Krenwinkel, and Van Houten, prosecutors had to convince the jury that although these women were under Manson's influence, they had carried out his orders willingly.

On July 24, 1970, in the courtroom of Judge Charles Older, the murder trial of Charles Manson, Susan Atkins, Patricia Krenwinkel, and Leslie Van Houten began. The previous night, Manson had carved an X into his forehead. Outside the Hall of Justice in Los Angeles, young female Family members—who would maintain a vigil throughout the long trial—passed out a typewritten statement from Manson explaining this sign: "I have X'd myself from your world. . . . You have created the monster. I am not of you, from you, nor do I condone your unjust attitude toward things, animals, and people that you do not try to understand." Soon the other defendants also burned X's into their foreheads.

Vincent Bugliosi's opening statement spelled out the essence of the prosecution's case. "The evidence will show Charles Manson to be a megalomaniac who coupled his insatiable thirst for power with an intense obsession for violent death," Bugliosi told the seven men and five women who had been selected for the jury.

Bugliosi tried to anticipate, and head off, any attempts on the part of the defendants to downplay their personal guilt:

> We anticipate that Mr. Manson, in his defense, will claim that neither he nor anyone else was the leader of the Family and that he never ordered anyone in the Family to do anything, much less commit these murders for him.

On the eve of the trial, Manson carved an X into his forehead, to signify that he had crossed himself out of the world of his accusers.

> We therefore intend to offer evidence at this trial showing that Charles Manson was in fact the dictatorial leader of the Family; that everyone in the Family was slavishly obedient to him; that he always had the other members of the Family do his bidding for him; and that eventually they committed the seven Tate-LaBianca murders at his command. . . .

> What about Charles Manson's followers, the other defendants in this case, Susan Atkins, Patricia Krenwinkel, and Leslie Van Houten?

> The evidence will show that they, along with Tex Watson, were the actual killers of the seven Tate-LaBianca victims.

> The evidence will also show that they were *very willing* participants in these mass murders, that by their overkill tactics—for instance, Rosemary LaBianca was stabbed forty-one times, Voytek Frykowski was stabbed fifty-one times, shot twice, and struck violently over the head thirteen times with the butt of a revolver—these defendants

Prosecutor Vincent Bugliosi speaks to reporters outside the courtroom. Bugliosi's careful and exhaustive presentation of the evidence established a bizarre motive for the gruesome crimes.

displayed that *even apart* from Charles Manson, murder ran through their own blood.

Bugliosi also offered something people had been looking for since the weekend of the gruesome murders: a motive. It was as bizarre as the crimes themselves.

Manson had read the Bible's Book of Revelation, which deals with the apocalypse—the cataclysmic struggle between good and evil that will usher in the second coming of Jesus Christ. In fact, at various times Manson had implied that *he* was Jesus Christ. Manson believed that the apocalypse was near and that it would be initiated by a race war during which black people would rise up and kill all the whites in the world. He referred to this war as Helter Skelter, a term that police had found written in blood (albeit misspelled) at the LaBianca house. Manson had taken the term from the title of a song on the White Album by the British rock group the Beatles. Manson felt that the Beatles were communicating directly with him through their music. In his view, lyrics from the song "Blackbird"—"All your life / You were only waiting for this moment to arise"— referred to black people rising up against whites. "Rise" had also been written in blood at the LaBianca house. Manson believed that the songs "Revolution 1" and "Revolution 9" referred to the Helter Skelter war as well, and that the song "Piggies"—"pigs" or "piggies" was Manson's term for the establishment—foretold the violent demise of whites. "Pig" had been written in blood at the Tate crime scene; "death to pigs," at the LaBianca crime scene.

How would Manson benefit from a race war? He and his followers were planning to hide in a "bottomless pit" in the desert until the war was over and the black people had won. Because blacks would prove incapable of ruling themselves, the Family believed, they would eventually turn to the last remaining whites—Manson and his followers, who would number 144,000, as predicted in the Book of Revelation—to lead them. Manson would thus become the ruler of the world.

There was only one problem: blacks hadn't started the Helter Skelter war. So Manson had staged the Tate and LaBianca murders, hoping that blacks would be blamed and that when whites retaliated, the conflict would begin. Throughout the trial, the prosecution would offer many witnesses to elucidate Manson's bizarre obsession with Helter Skelter.

The prosecution's star witness was Linda Kasabian. Kasabian's testimony got off to an incredibly strange

When former Family member Linda Kasabian (opposite page) raised her hand to be sworn in, Manson attorney Irving Kanarek (above) objected on the grounds that the witness was insane. Despite Kanarek's constant stream of objections, Kasabian proved to be the prosecution's most effective witness.

start. When the clerk asked her to raise her right hand to be sworn in, Manson's attorney, Irving Kanarek, shouted, "Object, Your Honor, on the grounds this witness is not competent and she is insane!" Kanarek would interrupt Kasabian's testimony with hundreds of frivolous objections on the first day alone—prompting Judge Older to find him in contempt of court and order him to spend the night in jail—but nothing shook Kasabian from the chilling story she told in a direct and soft-spoken manner. Kasabian described how Manson dominated the Family and controlled every aspect of his followers' lives. She described the two nights of carnage, including details only someone who had been there could know. On the second night, Kasabian had driven the car, but Manson had told her where to turn and where to stop, indicating that he alone was directing the Family's deadly mission.

Perhaps recognizing that Kasabian's testimony was so damning, Manson blurted out, "You've already told three lies."

From the witness stand Kasabian responded, "Oh, no, Charlie, I've spoken the truth, and you know it."

A growing realization that the case wasn't going his way was probably what prompted Manson on August 4 to hold up for the jury to see the front page of the *Los Angeles Times*, which Atkins's attorney had carelessly left on a table. The headline read, "Manson Guilty, Nixon Declares." President Nixon had offered his view on the trial to reporters the previous day, and Manson no doubt hoped that by showing the headline to the jurors, he could win a mistrial. After the jurors had been interviewed individually about their reaction, however, the judge ordered the trial to resume.

Later, Manson asked the judge to allow him to question one of the witnesses. When the judge refused, Manson sprang from his chair, leaped over the defense table, and landed a few feet from the judge's bench. In his hand he clutched a pencil, apparently intending to stab Judge Older with it. The court bailiff and two deputies fell on Manson and held him. As he was being taken from the courtroom, he screamed at the judge, "In the name of Christian justice, someone should cut your head off!"

Krenwinkel, Van Houten, and Atkins stood up and began chanting Latin phrases until the judge had them removed from the courtroom. When order was restored, all the defense attorneys moved for a mistrial. The judge replied, "It isn't going to be that easy. . . . They are not going to profit from their own wrong. . . . Denied."

Ronald Hughes, Van Houten's attorney, wasn't as lucky as Judge Older. Over the trial's Thanksgiving break, he went camping with two Manson Family members. He never returned. After he had been missing for two weeks, another attorney was appointed to represent Van Houten. Hughes's body was later found wedged between two boulders in a creek, a few miles from where he was last seen alive.

The prosecution's case took four months and included dozens of witnesses, ranging from forensic experts to Straight Satans motorcycle gang members to former Manson followers. Not only did Bugliosi pull together the evidentiary chain of events and provide numerous examples of Manson's domination of the Family, he also offered a host of witnesses to elucidate the bizarre Helter Skelter motive.

After the prosecution rested, the defense attorneys

At times the Manson girls (from left, Susan Atkins, Patricia Krenwinkel, and Leslie Van Houten) treated their murder trial as a lark, laughing, doodling, and interrupting the court proceedings with bizarre outbursts.

surprised the courtroom by announcing that the defense wouldn't present a case. That tactic usually means that the defense believes the prosecution hasn't met its burden of proof.

Kanarek, Manson's lawyer, took seven days to present a rambling summation. Of the four defense attorneys, Maxwell Keith, Van Houten's counsel, offered the most effective closing argument. Unlike the other defense lawyers, he attempted to place blame on Manson, arguing that his client couldn't be guilty of premeditated murder because her mind was totally controlled by Manson:

> The record discloses over and over again that all of these girls at the ranch believed Manson was God, really believed it.
>
> The record discloses that the girls obeyed his commands without any conscious questioning at all.

> If you believe the prosecution theory that these female defendants and Mr. Watson were extensions of Mr. Manson—his additional arms and legs as it were—if you believe that they were mindless robots, they cannot be guilty of premeditated murder. . . . [They] did not have minds to make up.

In the end, however, the jurors were unconvinced by this argument. After two days of deliberations, they decided that all four defendants were guilty of first-degree murder. During the penalty phase of the trial, Susan Atkins took the opportunity to accuse Linda Kasabian of masterminding the killings. Van Houten and Krenwinkel admitted they had participated in the killings but said that Manson had not. By now the jury was accustomed to such outlandish claims from the defendants. The jury gave all four defendants the death sentence.

The nine-and-a-half-month trial, the longest murder trial in American history to that point, was finally over. The jury had been sequestered for 225 days, another record.

In a separate trial, Charles "Tex" Watson was also convicted and sentenced to death for the murders. But in 1972 the state of California abolished the death penalty, and all five sentences were commuted to life in prison.

Atkins, Krenwinkel, Van Houten, and Watson have all renounced Manson and his philosophy. As for the man who inspired and ordered the two nights of murder, he too remains incarcerated, his vision of Helter Skelter yet to come to pass.

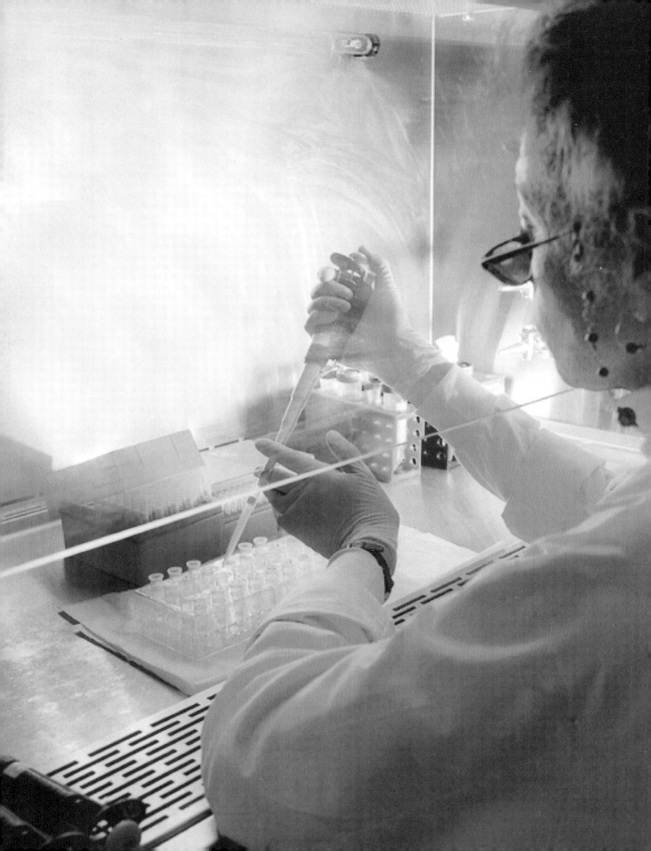

BEYOND A REASONABLE DOUBT

A lab technician prepares samples for DNA analysis. The development of DNA fingerprinting has proved to be an invaluable aid for law enforcement and prosecutors.

To obtain a criminal conviction in the American system of justice, prosecutors must establish the defendant's guilt beyond a reasonable doubt. This standard of proof is high, and for good reason. It helps protect the innocent from being wrongfully convicted.

To fulfill their high burden of proof, good prosecutors strive to present the jury with as complete a picture of the crime as possible. To do this, they try to incorporate various kinds of evidence, including what is known as real, or physical, evidence. Physical evidence is any tangible object, such as a weapon, fingerprint, or bloodstain.

Science has played a crucial role in the use of this kind of evidence. The past 100 years, in particular, have seen revolutionary advances in scientific techniques for collecting and analyzing physical evidence. This has had a major impact on police work: criminals who in the past would have escaped justice are now apprehended. For example, a national repository for fingerprint records, first established in 1924, made it possible to identify a suspect using a unique characteristic he or she left at a crime scene. The ability to establish blood type (A, B, AB, or O) from a crime-scene sample, while it could never point to a single possible perpetrator, enabled investigators both to rule out certain suspects and to identify others who warranted additional scrutiny. A further advance permitted blood to be tested for genetic markers, enzymes and proteins that vary from person to person. Everyone's blood contains an enzyme known as PGM, for example, but there are at least 10 distinct subtypes of that enzyme. The odds are pretty good that two blood samples with even three or four identical genetic markers came from the same person.

If these and other scientific advances in evidence collection and analysis have aided police in catching criminals, they have also made it possible for prosecutors to present more-airtight cases. Of course, science has also raised the bar for prosecutors because many jurors now expect that scientific evidence will be presented at trial. Plus, defense attorneys have access to sophisticated science as well, and any inconsistencies or perceived inconsistencies in the scientific evidence presented by a prosecutor can lead to acquittal. At the very least, an effective prosecutor must be familiar with the basics of forensic science. He or she must be able to present the scientific evidence gathered by law enforcement in a way that jurors can understand.

Occasionally a prosecution goes beyond that, using forensic science that even the police are unfamiliar with to convict a criminal. In 1988 two farsighted prosecutors in Florida turned to a scientific tool that had never before been used in an American criminal courtroom. That tool has since become a mainstay of physical evidence, establishing the guilt—or innocence—of thousands of suspects beyond a reasonable doubt.

The Florida case began after midnight on May 9,

1986. A 27-year-old Orlando resident named Nancy Hodge was taking out her contact lenses in her bathroom when she heard a noise. She turned to see a man in the hallway. For about six seconds the intruder's face was in full light.

The man knocked Hodge to the floor and beat her. Then he covered her face and raped her three times. Afterward he wiped the semen from her body and checked every room to make sure he had left no evidence.

In spite of the rapist's attempt to avoid leaving evidence, a vaginal swab yielded a sample of his semen. In addition, Hodge was able to provide a description of her attacker, though the police sketch didn't lead to the arrest of a suspect.

Soon, however, Orlando police became convinced that the Hodge case wasn't an isolated incident. Other rapes, particularly in the southeastern part of the city, displayed a similar modus operandi. The attacks always occurred in the victim's home, and after midnight, when she might be asleep. The rapist always covered the victim's eyes to prevent her from identifying him. The rapist carried a knife. In most cases, he took the victim's driver's license.

By early 1987, Orlando police had linked the same man to 7 rapes (ultimately, as many as 23 sexual assaults would be attributed to him), in addition to numerous break-ins and instances of prowling. Detectives began piecing together a profile of the perpetrator. He stalked the women and knew their schedules and living patterns. And he was exceedingly careful not to leave evidence at the crime scenes.

Finally, however, the rapist got careless. After one rape was reported, police found fingerprints on the frame of the screen window where the attacker had entered the victim's residence. Also, a vaginal swab from that victim produced a reliable semen sample.

The Orlando Police Department put its search into

high gear. Plainclothes police staked out neighbor-hoods and patrolled the streets in unmarked cars. In little more than a week, they received a phone call from a woman reporting a prowler. Responding to that call, officers saw a blue 1979 Ford Granada whose dri-ver was apparently trying to flee the area. The police gave chase, apprehending the suspect when his car crashed into a utility pole. The suspect's name was Tommie Lee Andrews.

On the afternoon of March 1, some eight months after she had been attacked, police brought Hodge to the police station to view a lineup. She immediately picked Andrews out of the group. Police charged him with a list of crimes: rape, armed burglary, sexual bat-tery, and aggravated battery.

Tim Berry, an Orange County assistant state's attor-ney, drew the assignment of prosecuting Andrews. An experienced prosecutor, Berry knew that it would be a tough case. Only one victim, Nancy Hodge, had seen and could positively identify Andrews. And while the semen samples recovered from two of the victims fit Andrews's blood type, they also fit that of 30 percent of all American men. Berry wanted to put together an ironclad case against Andrews, but short of developing new evidence, that didn't seem possible.

Five months after Berry received the case, a col-league stumbled upon a way new evidence might indeed be developed. Jeffrey Ashton, also an assistant state's attorney, had seen a news report about a new method of identification known as DNA (or genetic) fingerprinting. Like blood-typing, the method would allow a sample recovered at a crime scene to be com-pared with a sample taken from a known suspect. But DNA fingerprinting could yield a much more conclu-sive match: whereas blood-typing might enable 70 per-cent of the population to be excluded as the possible source of a crime-scene sample, DNA fingerprinting held out the possibility that virtually everyone except a particular suspect could be excluded. It could, in other words, remove all reasonable doubt from a juror's mind.

The trouble was, DNA fingerprinting remained virtually unknown outside a tiny circle of geneticists. American law enforcement agencies didn't use it to solve crimes, no American prosecutor had ever introduced it into a courtroom, and even among scientists few could give the most basic explanation of how it worked—let alone explain it in enough detail to persuade a jury.

DNA—deoxyribonucleic acid—is a large, two-stranded, spiral-shaped molecule found in the nuclei of cells. Each strand comprises a long chain of nucleotides, chemical compounds made up in part of four bases: adenine (A), thymine (T), cytosine (C), and guanine (G). These bases are the building blocks of the genetic code, which is passed on from parents to offspring and determines the physical structure, characteristics, and development of all cellular organisms. The code itself resides in the particular sequence of the nucleotide "letters" A, T, C, and G.

Genetically normal humans have 46 chromosomes, half inherited from each parent. These chromosomes carry our genes, segments of DNA that consist of a specific sequence of letters that control the production of a particular protein. The entire human genetic code contains 30,000 to 40,000 genes and about 3 billion separate nucleotide letters.

A large part of the genetic code is similar for everyone because all humans share countless characteristics—the qualities that separate us from the other species. But within the 3-billion-letter sequence are about 10 million spots where the letters can vary from person to person. Variable segments of DNA, which are called polymorphic segments or genetic markers, account for our individual characteristics. Except for identical twins, no two people share the exact same genetic code.

Like many scientific advances, DNA fingerprinting was discovered largely by accident. In 1984 an English scientist named Alec Jeffreys, working at Leicester University, was studying how genes evolve. Dr. Jeffreys wanted to examine areas where the genetic sequence varies widely from person to person. He developed radioactive probes that would attach to such areas after he had cut the DNA using enzymes. After the pieces were aligned according to length on a sheet of gel, he took an X-ray photo. The DNA pieces that the radioactive probes had attached to—areas of great genetic variability—showed up as dark bands of varying widths. The entire X-ray photo resembled a merchandise bar code.

Jeffreys made two important discoveries about these DNA prints, as they came to be called. First, DNA extracted from any type of cell—blood, skin, sperm, bone—from the same person produces an identical print. Second, each person has a unique DNA print.

Because Jeffreys's genetic fingerprinting could reveal family relationships, paternity testing (establishing whether a particular man is a child's biological father) became an obvious early application. But English police soon contacted the scientist in the hopes that he could help them solve a crime.

In a small village in the English countryside, a girl had been raped and murdered years before. Although a man had confessed to the crime, the police harbored doubts that he was the actual perpetrator, because a similar crime had recently been committed in the same area while the suspect was in police custody. Jeffreys ran a genetic fingerprint test on samples from the crime scenes and the suspect. The tests proved that the suspect wasn't the killer in either case.

With their investigation at a dead end, police took an extraordinary step: they obtained a court order to get blood samples from every man between the age of 16 and 34 who lived in the rural area where the mur-

ders had occurred. A genetic fingerprint test would be run on each sample.

While the testing was being done, the police heard of a man who said that an acquaintance, Colin Pitchfork, had persuaded him to provide a blood sample in Pitchfork's name. Pitchfork claimed that he couldn't provide his own blood sample because he had a history of indecent exposure and the police would try to frame him. Both men were arrested, and Pitchfork's blood sample was rushed to Jeffreys's laboratory. Although it had taken police 4,583 blood samples to find their suspect, Pitchfork's was an absolute match and he confessed.

British geneticist Alec Jeffreys (right) developed the technique of genetic finger-printing in 1984.

SIX PROBE MATCH

Profile 1

Profile 2

Profile 3

Victim Suspect Evidence

Victim Suspect Evidence

Victim Suspect Evidence

Profile 4

Profile 5

Profile 6

Victim Suspect Evidence

Victim Suspect Evidence

Victim Suspect Evidence

DNA results from a rape case. Note that for each segment of DNA tested, the dark bands of the suspect's sample align perfectly with dark bands from the evidence sample. This means that the semen collected after the crime almost certainly came from the suspect.

When he heard a news report about the incident in England, Orlando assistant state's attorney Jeffrey Ashton recognized that DNA fingerprinting might make the rape case against Tommie Lee Andrews.

"I thought to myself: 'That's fascinating!'" Ashton remembered. " 'Wouldn't it be great if it could be done here?' And shortly afterward, purely by accident, I was looking through the *Florida Bar News* and I saw an ad from the Lifecodes Laboratory in Valhalla, N.Y., that advertised DNA paternity testing.

"I called them up and they told me they had just branched into forensics, and it kind of snowballed from there. It was just a lucky series of happenstances."

Ashton and the other prosecutor on the Andrews case, Tim Berry, called Michael Baird, the director of forensic and paternity testing at Lifecodes, and asked if he would analyze the evidence in the upcoming rape trial. The evidence was flown to the Lifecodes laboratory in upstate New York. When the DNA print from Andrews's blood sample was compared with the prints from semen samples recovered from the rape victims, the genetic bar codes matched band for band. According to the Lifecodes database, the frequency of Andrews's DNA pattern was 1 in 10 billion. Because the earth's population is slightly more than 5 billion, Andrews was the only human being who matched the print.

In theory this evidence should have been totally conclusive. But Berry knew that because DNA fingerprinting had never been used in court, Andrews's attorneys would challenge it. And because the technology was new and highly complex, being able to explain how it worked in terms the jurors could understand would be crucial. Before the trial started, Berry needed to learn everything he could about the scientific background for DNA testing. He arranged for a member of his staff to meet with David Housman, a molecular biologist at the Massachusetts Institute of Technology, to take a crash course in genetics. Berry planned to use Housman as an expert witness.

James Valerino, the defense lawyer representing Tommie Lee Andrews, recognized that the evidence was overwhelmingly against his client. "When we first got our witness list, we saw all these experts the state was going to use," Valerino said. "We looked for somebody to assist us. We just came up against a stone wall. This was so new, we didn't even know where to go to find anybody."

Valerino continued, "So we ended up calling the state's experts and asked them if there were other people in the country we could talk to. They gave us some names. When we talked with those people, and told them who the state's DNA witness was, they said, 'Well, he's the best. What he says is gospel.' And I thought: Geez, what do we do?"

When a new type of technology is used as evidence in a court case, the scientific test must meet what is called the Frye standard. This term means that the judge believes the technology is "sufficiently established to have gained general acceptance in the particular field in which it belongs."

The judge held a pretrial hearing to consider the new technology. Berry called his expert witness Housman, and the judge ruled that DNA evidence was admissible. The next day the jury of two women and four men was seated.

Housman's expert testimony walked the jury through the basic genetic lesson he had given the attorneys before the trial and the judge during the pretrial hearing. Then Hodge took the stand and was asked to identify her assailant. Nervously, she indicated Andrews.

The next day, the Lifecodes geneticists were put on the stand. They explained how the samples were taken from Andrews and showed the jury the actual DNA patterns on a lighted background. The jurors could see for themselves that Andrews's blood sample matched the DNA evidence at the crime scene.

When Berry asked the witness to explain the statistical numbers that proved Andrews could be the only match, Andrews's lawyers objected. Berry was stunned. He had anticipated challenges to the admissibility of DNA fingerprinting but hadn't expected the statistical evidence the tests generated to be questioned. With no legal argument prepared to defend the statistics, Berry decided to withdraw the question. It cost him the trial. The jury deadlocked and the judge declared a mistrial. The airtight evidence had not convinced the jury after all.

Before Berry had a chance to retry the Hodge rape case, Andrews was scheduled to stand trial for the second rape with which he had been charged. In the two weeks between trials, Berry and Ashton did more research and established a legal precedent that used statistical evidence to bolster forensic evidence. This time the DNA evidence was accepted. Also, the evidence included the two fingerprints from the victim's window-screen frame. The jury

Rapist guilty, gets prison in 2nd DNA trial

By Roger Roy

OF THE SENTINEL STAFF

A suspect in several rapes whose trials were the first in which genetic comparison tests were used as evidence was convicted Friday in Orange Circuit Court and sentenced to prison.

Minutes after the six-member jury found Tommy Lee Andrews guilty of rape, aggravated battery and burglary, Circuit Judge Rom Powell sentenced Andrews to 22 years.

Andrews, 23, is scheduled for trial later this month on three more rape charges. Police said he is a suspect in a dozen other rapes.

Andrews was convicted Friday of attacking an Orlando woman in her home in February. The victim could not identify her attacker.

However, testimony showed that two of Andrews' fingerprints were on the frame of a screen from a window the rapist used to enter the house.

Several experts testified that a test that compares genetic molecules from a rapist's semen with the molecule from a suspect's blood showed that Andrews was the attacker.

That test had been admitted as evidence only once before — a trial for Andrews in which he was accused of raping another woman.

Andrews' first case ended in a mistrial two weeks ago when jurors could not reach a verdict. During that trial, the victim identified Andrews as her attacker. However, police found no fingerprints to implicate Andrews.

Andrews, a former pharmaceutical clerk, is scheduled to be retried on that charge later.

In both trials, jurors heard evidence that Lifecodes Inc., a New York research lab, had compared the genetic molecules from Andrews with the rapist's semen.

The witnesses, who included Lifecodes scientists and a well-known Massachusetts Institute of Technology biologist who has no connections with the company, said the test has been accepted in scientific circles for about 10 years. But it had never been used as evidence in a criminal trial.

In the test, deoxyribonucleic acid, or DNA, is extracted chemically from the semen and the suspect's blood. Fragments of DNA are then compared.

Because DNA, which is found in all cells in the body, is different in everyone except identical twins, an exact match of the DNA comparison is a virtual "fingerprint" identification, prosecutors Jeff Ashton and Tim Berry said.

But in closing arguments Friday morning, defense attorneys Hal Uhrig and James Valerino told jurors that the DNA tests are too new and unproven.

Uhrig said later developments may show the test to be unsound.

"In 1969, we put a man on the moon, contrary to the scientific beliefs of not too many years before," Uhrig said.

Ashton, however, told jurors that the new tests are even more reliable than eyewitness accounts.

"The only people who haven't accepted these tests are those two attorneys right there who are defending their client," Ashton said.

A headline from the Orlando Sentinel announces the results of the groundbreaking Andrews case.

convicted Andrews, and he was sentenced to 22 years in prison.

Andrews was also retried in the rape of Hodge. Even though Andrews's girlfriend and her sister backed his alibi that he had been home throughout the evening of the crime, the jury wasn't buying it.

Housman gave his expert testimony again, leading one juror to say, "We all felt like we were back in science class." Then Lifecodes witness Michael Baird testified, and the question of statistical evidence was brought up. Andrews's lawyers tried to question the reliability of the test on the grounds that not all of Andrews's DNA had been tested. But Baird explained that the only DNA that mattered were the variable parts.

After deliberating for 90 minutes, the jury returned a guilty verdict. Andrews received a 78-year sentence. Combined with his sentence from the other rape trial, he faced 100 years behind bars. Thanks in large part to the pioneering use of DNA fingerprinting, the serial rapist would be off the streets for a long time.

Since Tommie Lee Andrews became the first American convicted with DNA evidence, the scientific test has been used in thousands of criminal investigations. The FBI has developed a national computerized network—called the Combined DNA Index System (CODIS)—that links state databases containing the DNA fingerprints of convicted sex criminals and other violent offenders. CODIS has helped law enforcement solve crimes that would otherwise have gone unsolved.

As Attorney General Janet Reno said, "Our system of criminal justice is best described as a search for the truth. Increasingly, the forensic use of DNA technology is an important ally in that search."

♣   ♣   ♣

In one sense, any prosecution that leads to the conviction of a guilty defendant could be termed "great":

the goal of the criminal justice system is, after all, justice. Yet certain cases are unusually difficult to prosecute and involve evil of great magnitude. In those instances only the ingenuity, skill, and tenacity of a prosecutor stand between society and a dangerous offender.

Further Reading

Bergreen, Laurence. *Capone: The Man and the Era*. New York: Simon & Schuster, 1996.

Bugliosi, Vincent, and Curt Gentry. *Helter Skelter*. New York: Bantam Books, 1974.

DeLaughter, Bobby. *Never Too Late: The Prosecutor's Story of Justice in the Medgar Evers Case*. New York: Scribner, 2001.

Knappman, Edward W. *Great American Trials*. Detroit: Visible Ink Press, 1994.

Nickell, Joe, and John F. Fischer. *Crime Science*. Lexington: The University of Kentucky Press, 1999.

Persico, Joseph E. *Nuremberg Infamy on Trial*. New York: Penguin Books, 1995.

Taylor, Telford. *The Anatomy of the Nuremberg Trials*. New York: Knopf, 1992.

Vollers, Maryanne. *Ghosts of Mississippi*. Boston: Little, Brown, 1995.

Index

Index

Picture Credits

NANCY PEACOCK is the author of three other Chelsea House books: *Dave Thomas* in the OVERCOMING ADVERSITY series; and *Drowning Our Sorrows: Psychological Effects of Alcohol Abuse* and *Alcohol* in the JUNIOR DRUG AWARENESS series. She has written travel books, and her articles and columns have appeared in *BusinessWeek, New Choices, Midwest Living, Romantic Homes, Cleveland Magazine*, and many other periodicals. She lives in Medina, Ohio, with her husband, Larry, and two children, Aaron and Natalie.

AUSTIN SARAT is William Nelson Cromwell Professor of Jurisprudence and Political Science at Amherst College, where he also chairs the Department of Law, Jurisprudence and Social Thought. Professor Sarat is the author or editor of 23 books and numerous scholarly articles. Among his books are *Law's Violence, Sitting in Judgment: Sentencing the White Collar Criminal*, and *Justice and Injustice in Law and Legal Theory*. He has received many academic awards and held several prestigious fellowships. He is President of the Law & Society Association and Chair of the Working Group on Law, Culture and the Humanities. In addition, he is a nationally recognized teacher and educator whose teaching has been featured in the *New York Times*, on the *Today* show, and on National Public Radio's *Fresh Air*.